PRINCESS PRINCESS
Princess·Princess
2
MIKIYO TSUDA
DMP DIGITAL MANGA PUBLISHING

CONTENTS

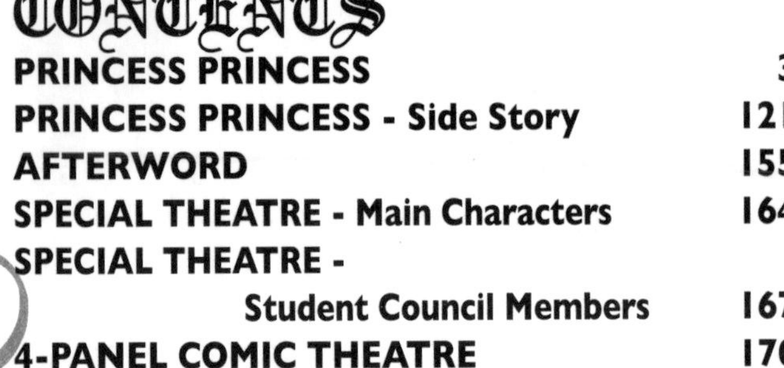

The Story So Far...

Tohru Kouno transferred to an all boys school and received a very warm welcome. He soon discovered that his new school has a "Princess System" where a select few students dress up as girls to give the rest of the guys an outlet for their frustrations. Tohru is selected, and tempted by many perks of the job, agrees to become a princess alongside Shihoudani and Mikoto...

Translation	*Earl Gertwagen*
Lettering	*Geoff Porter*
Graphic Design	*Daryl Kuxhouse*
Editing	*Daryl Kuxhouse*
Editor in Chief	*Fred Lui*
Publisher	*Hikaru Sasahara*

English Edition Published by
DIGITAL MANGA PUBLISHING
A division of DIGITAL MANGA, Inc.
1487 W 178th Street, Suite 300
Gardena, CA 90248

www.dmpbooks.com

First Edition: February 2007
ISBN-10: 1-56970-855-X
ISBN-13: 978-1-56970-855-2

1 3 5 7 9 10 8 6 4 2

Printed in China

プリンセス・プリンセス
PRINCESS・PRINCESS

TOHRU-CHAN! I CAME TO SEE Y--

SAYAKA!

WHAT ARE YOU DOING HERE? DIDN'T THEY TELL YOU TO STAY AWAY FROM ME?!

TOHRU-CHAN...

I COMPLETELY FORGOT! I'M STILL WEARING MY PRINCESS OUTFIT!!
KSHHHHHHHHH
GOTHIC LOLITA CLOTHES
OH! UHH... THIS IS...
OH, THIS?
WOOP
AS YOU CAN SEE, THE TWO OF US ARE DRESSED IN THE SAME OUTFIT.
WE'RE ACTUALLY WEARING THESE COSTUMES AS PART OF A SCHOOL EVENT THIS VERY MOMENT.
OH... YOU ARE...?
ARE THEY BOTH... BOYS?

WHAT ARE YOU DOING HERE? WHAT ABOUT SCHOOL?! AREN'T YOU SUPPOSED TO BE IN CLASS RIGHT NOW? YOU DIDN'T DITCH SCHOOL SO YOU COULD COME HERE, DID YOU?!

I DIDN'T DITCH! WE FINISHED EXAMS AND WE'RE ON VACATION!!

THAT'S NOT THE ISSUE HERE!

KOUNO!

I WENT AND BORROWED THE KEY TO THE CLUBHOUSE FROM THE STUDENT COUNCIL. WHY DON'T YOU COOL OFF AND TALK PRIVATELY IN THERE?
JINGLE
ちゃり…
I CAN SEE THIS IS IMPORTANT.
SAKA-MOTO ...

THANKS, SAKAMOTO... FOR GOING OUT OF YOUR WAY LIKE THAT...
I RAN OFF WITHOUT SAYING ANYTHING...
OH, THAT'S OKAY. I THOUGHT IT MIGHT HELP, SO I DECIDED TO GO GET IT MYSELF.
ALL RIGHT... WELL...
SINCE YOU OFFERED ...
HAH HAH...
AH!
BUT WE'RE WORKING RIGHT NOW...
OR WE WERE...
WHAT DO WE DO...?

AH. IN THAT CASE, FOR KOUNO TO BE ABLE TO SLIP AWAY AND TALK, WE'LL HAVE SHIHOUDANI AND MIKOTO GO BACK TO WORK...
YOU BETTER HURRY BACK, SINCE THE CROWD WAS GETTING RESTLESS WONDERING WHERE YOU WENT.
CAN YOU TWO PLEASE KEEP WATCH AROUND HERE?
AND PLEASE KEEP WHAT HAPPENED HERE CONFIDENTIAL.
てきぱきてきぱき
INSTRUCT
INSTRUCT
YEAH, OKAY. SURE...
WE'LL BE OFF.
SAKAMOTO-SAMA...
IF YOU DON'T WANT TO BE THE NEXT PRESIDENT, YOU BETTER NOT LET ARISADA SEE YOU HANDLING THINGS SO WELL.
BUT THANKS ALL THE SAME...
WHAT? WHY...?
OH...

I JUST ACTED EXACTLY HOW THE PRESIDENT WANTS ME TO...
DIDN'T I...?
I KNEW YOU WERE GOOD, SAKAMOTO-SAMA!! YOU'D BE PERFECT AS PRESIDENT! I *MUST* HAVE YOU! ♡
FHN
HN
HN
IMPECCABLY!
HIS MASTERY OF GIVING COMMANDS... HIS CAREFUL CONSIDERATION OF THE SITUATION... I COULD ALMOST HEAR THAT CREEPY SUPPRESSED LAUGH OF HIS...
NO KIDDING...
WELL, WE WON'T GET ANYTHING DONE JUST STANDING HERE. LET'S DO WHAT HE SAYS.

THE ONLY PROBLEM IS THAT MIKOTO-KUN WILL BE LEFT ALL BY HIMSELF...

AH!

OH YEAH!

ぶる TREMBLE

ぶる TREMBLE

SO THAT MEANS ...

THAT MEANS I HAVE TO WALK AROUND LIKE THIS ALONE ...?

ぶる TREMBLE

NOOOOOO!!

IF I DON'T HAVE YOU GUYS AS A SHIELD WHILE I WALK AROUND, WHAT'S GOING TO HAPPEN TO ME?!

THEY'LL BE ALL OVER ME!

MIKOTO...

SO THAT'S WHAT YOU THINK ABOUT US, IS IT?

HNNN
フウ…
SINCE THIS IS MY FAULT…
…FINE.

SORRY SAKAMOTO, BUT CAN YOU STAY WITH MIKOTO WHILE WE'RE GONE?
I KNOW YOU'RE BUSY…
SURE… THAT'S FINE.

THERE. NOW YOUR PERSONAL SAFETY IS ENSURED.
HUH?
PAT
ポンッ
HOW DOES JUST HAVING SAKAMOTO ENSURE MY PERSONAL SAFETY?!

WHAT ARE YOU TALKING ABOUT? IF YOU WALK AROUND WITH THIS THING HERE, NO ONE WILL LAY A FINGER ON YOU. CROWDS WILL PUSH AND SHOVE EACH OTHER TO MAKE A PATH! BEHOLD, THE SAKAMOTO BADGE!
SERIOUSLY! I SAW IT!
"THIS THING"…?
IT… IT'LL REALLY HAVE THAT EFFECT…?

WELL, WE'LL GET GOING, THEN. LEAVE THINGS TO US.

SORRY, SAKAMOTO...

THANKS.

HUFF

ALL RIGHT,

WE SHOULD GET GOING, TOO...

SO JUST TO GET THINGS STRAIGHT... HOW DO YOU KNOW THIS GIRL, TOHRU?

THIS IS SAYAKA...
SHE'S... MY LITTLE SISTER...

I'M NOT YOUR SISTER!
きっ
GLARE

I DON'T THINK OF YOU AS MY BROTHER!!
BUT WE GREW UP TOGETHER JUST LIKE SIBLINGS DO.
FWIP
YOU'RE MY COUSIN SO WE'RE STILL RELATED, BUT WE'RE NOT REAL SIBLINGS!!

BUT ISN'T THIS YOUR FAULT?!

LUNGE

YOU MOVED OUT OF THE HOUSE AND CHANGED SCHOOLS WHILE I WAS STILL AT THE HOSPITAL!!

AND I THOUGHT YOU'D COME HOME FOR VACATION, BUT THEN I HEAR YOU'RE STAYING IN THE DORMS!

HOW DID YOU...?

PLEASE COME BACK HOME, TOHRU-KUN. COME BACK TO YOUR OLD SCHOOL!
I DON'T WANT TO LIVE A LIFE THAT DOESN'T HAVE YOU IN IT!
I DON'T THINK OF YOU AS ANYTHING BUT MY SISTER...
AND I WON'T BE GOING HOME UNTIL YOU THINK OF ME AS YOUR BROTHER...
NO! IF YOU'RE MY BROTHER THEN WE CAN'T BE LOVERS! WE WON'T BE ABLE TO GET MARRIED EITHER! I DON'T WANT THAT!!
EVER SINCE I WAS LITTLE, IT WAS ALWAYS MY DREAM TO BECOME YOUR WIFE.
I STILL LOVED YOU EVEN THOUGH I KNEW AS SIBLINGS WE COULD NEVER GET MARRIED!
WHEN I FOUND OUT YOU WEREN'T MY REAL BROTHER, I WAS SO HAPPY I COULD'VE DIED!!
TWITCH
JUST LOVE ME BACK! AS A LOVER AND NOT AS YOUR SISTER!
THIS GIRL... IS SO INSEN-SITIVE...
DOESN'T SHE UNDER-STAND WHAT SHE'S SAYING?

OH! OR MAYBE YOU'RE RESTRAINING YOURSELF BECAUSE IT WOULD BE HARD ON MOM AND DAD?
I KNOW YOU'RE EARNEST, SO I THOUGHT MAYBE THAT'S WHY!
SHE ONLY THINKS OF HERSELF...
SAYAKA ... THAT'S NOT...
AND IF WE GOT MARRIED, TOGETHER WITH MY MOM AND DAD, WE COULD BE A REAL FAMILY! THAT SHOULD MAKE YOU HAPPY SINCE YOU DON'T HAVE ANY PARENTS!!
BELIEVING THAT HER VALUES ARE FLAWLESS,
SHE FORCES THEM ON HIM.
JUST LOOKING AT HER IRRITATES ME.
I BETTER GO LET YOUR MOM KNOW.
NO! IF YOU DON'T SAY YOU'RE COMING HOME, I WON'T FORGIVE YOU!!

EXCUSE ME, BUT...

ZZZUT

ACK!

NO MATTER HOW HARD YOU TRY, IT WON'T WORK.

WH... WHAT IS IT? WHAT DO YOU MEAN...?

YUUJIROU ...?

THIS IS A LITTLE SECRET, BUT YOUR BROTHER ISN'T THE TYPE OF PERSON THAT'S INTERESTED IN GIRLS.

IN OTHER WORDS... ***YOUR BROTHER IS GAY.***

SLIDE

HE WAS STILL YOUNG, AND WAS STRUGGLING TO ACCEPT HIMSELF AND HIS SEXUAL INCLINATION.

BUT NOW, THANKS TO ME - *HIS LOVER* - HE'S COME TO BE ABLE TO ACCEPT THE WAY HE IS!

KISSSSSSS

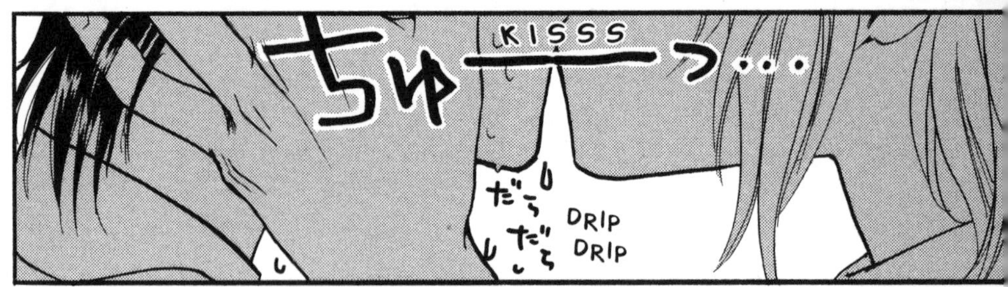

— ONE MINUTE LATER... —

NGHAA!
HEH
WELL? STILL DON'T BELIEVE ME?
GATAK
IF NOT, WE CAN CONTINUE...
INCH
NO... NO, IT'S NOT TRUE...
HE... TOHRU-KUN DOESN'T--

ぱたぱたぱた
BTAP
BTAP
BTAP
IT'S NOT TRUUUUUUE!!
バタ―ン
WHAM

YU-

YUUJI-ROOOU...
WHAT DO YOU THINK YOU'RE DOING...
WHAT? SHE WENT HOME, DIDN'T SHE? ISN'T THAT WHAT YOU WANTED?

WHAT I... WHAT I WANTED WAS--
BUT THAT WAS ONLY A TEMPORARY SOLUTION.
HUH...?

SHE'S STUNNED FROM THE RAW KISS WE SHOWED HER, BUT WHEN SHE RECOVERS FROM HER SHOCK AND CALMS DOWN, SHE'LL SURELY RETURN. SHE DIDN'T GET WHAT SHE WANTED.
YOU'LL HAVE TO BE PREPARED FOR THE NEXT TIME SHE COMES.

THE NEXT TIME...

WE'LL HAVE TO SHOW HER MORE THAN JUST A KISS. WHAT SHOULD WE DO?

HMM... THIS IS ROUGH...

YUUJIROU...

WAAAAH
BAM
BAM
WAAAAH
TWEEEEET
YOU'RE GOING TO GO RIGHT BACK TO WORK?
YOU SHOULDN'T FEEL OBLIGATED. EVERYTHING SHOULD BE TAKEN CARE OF.
WE EVEN LEFT SAKAMOTO-SAMA WITH HIM.
BUT IT'S MY FAULT THEY HAVE TO TAKE CARE OF IT THEMSELVES, SO... I'LL FEEL BAD IF I DON'T.

YOU'RE SO CONSCIENTIOUS. YOU LOOK SHALLOW, BUT YOU'RE ACTUALLY QUITE A CONSIDERATE GUY.
SIGH
IT'S NOTHING LIKE THAT...

WAAAAAH
TWEEET
CHATTER
CHATTER
CHATTER
CHATTER
WE LEFT SAKAMOTO WITH HIM SO IT SHOULD BE FINE, BUT I WONDER IF MIKOTO'S DOING OKAY...
HOPEFULLY HE HASN'T GONE NUTS FROM THE ATTENTION.
PEER
PEER
WHERE IS HE?
AH! THERE THEY ARE!
...BUT...

AMAZING... THERE'S AN INVISIBLE BARRIER SURROUNDING THEM...
THEY EVEN HAVE CHAIRS...
I KNEW SAKAMOTO WOULD HAVE A POWERFUL EFFECT BUT... THAT'S INCREDIBLE...
IT'S LIKE A SCHOOL OF TUNA PARTING FOR A HUNGRY DOLPHIN...
HUGE SCHOOL OF TUNA
DOLPHIN
THEY LOOK LIKE GIRL'S DAY DOLLS DRESSED LIKE THAT NEXT TO EACH OTHER.
ESPECIALLY WITH THE RAGING MASSES AROUND THEM...
ぷっ
PFF
>HA HA< IF YOU SAID THAT TO MIKOTO... HE'D GET SO MAD.
THE PRINCESSES ARE ALL HERE!
THE OTHERS!
WAAH
CHATTER
ざわっ
CHATTER
ざわっ
CHATTER
ざわっ
CHATTER
AH!

HEY, MIKOTO! SORRY TO LEAVE YOU WITH ALL THE WORK.
GATAK
KOUNO!

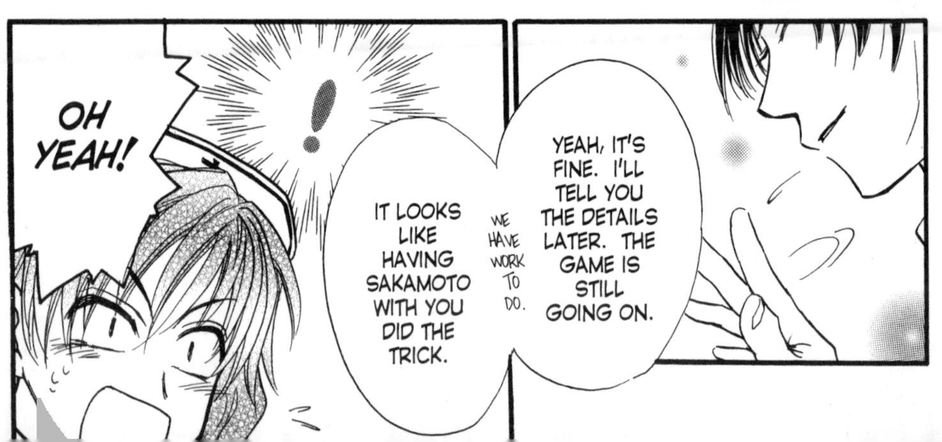

IT WAS AMAZING! THE CROWD OPENED UP A PATH LIKE THAT ONE SCENE IN THE TEN COMMANDMENTS! AND THEN WITHOUT EVEN BEING ASKED, THEY BROUGHT US CHAIRS! IT REALLY *IS* LIKE A SAKAMOTO BADGE!

WHEN HE PARTS THE SEA.

SPREAD

WAHH!

OH, IT'S SAKAMOTO-SAMA.

HEY, SOMEONE BRING CHAIRS!

GIVE HIM ROOM!

HEEEY!

HI, SAKAMOTO-SAMA!

ISN'T IT?! EVERYTHING IN FRONT OF YOU JUST STARTS TO OPEN UP!

YEAH! YEAH!

UMM...

FORGET THE TEN COMMANDMENTS...THE THREE OF YOU TOGETHER MAKE A CRATER SO BIG THEY HAD TO ***STOP THE GAME...***

BACK AWAY

ざわっ
CHATTER
ざわ
CHATTER
ざわっ
CHATTER
キーンコーンカーンコーン…
DIIING DOOONG… DIIING DOOONG…
キーンコーン…
DING DOONG…
カーン…
DING
コーン…
DOONG…
SO SAYAKA... THAT GIRL THAT SUDDENLY SHOWED UP TODAY...
IS MY LITTLE SISTER...
BUT SHE'S TECHNICALLY MY COUSIN.

ACTUALLY, MY PARENTS BOTH DIED JUST AFTER I STARTED ELEMENTARY SCHOOL.
WHAT...?
THEN I WAS TAKEN IN BY MY AUNT AND UNCLE... SAYAKA'S PARENTS...
I WAS STILL YOUNG. AND I KNEW THEY WEREN'T SOME RANDOM STRANGERS...
SO WE STARTED GETTING ALONG PRETTY QUICKLY.
BUT SAYAKA...
MY LITTLE SISTER... FOR SOME REASON STARTED GETTING REALLY POSSESSIVE,
AND WOULD SCARE OFF ALL THE PEOPLE WHO WERE CLOSE TO ME. SHE EVEN CUT ONE OF THEM WITH A KNIFE ONCE.

I FIGURED I COULDN'T GO ON LIVING WITH HER, SO I DECIDED TO MOVE OUT HERE WITHOUT TELLING HER.
OH, WOW...
TO THINK YOU HAD SUCH A ROUGH PAST... I HAD NO IDEA, KOUNO.
YOU AND SHIHOUDANI ARE ALWAYS SO HYPER...
SO THE REASON WHY YOU JUMPED ON THOSE PRINCESS BENEFITS WASN'T BECAUSE YOU WANTED THE MONEY, BUT BECAUSE YOU WANTED TO BE AS LITTLE OF A BURDEN ON YOUR FAMILY AS POSSIBLE?
YEAH. THEY WERE KIND ENOUGH TO TAKE ME IN AND IT ONLY BROUGHT THEM TROUBLE.
I DON'T WANT TO DO MORE DAMAGE THAN I ALREADY HAVE.
THAT'S LIKE YOU...
SO KOUNO WASN'T DOING IT FOR THE MONEY...
AFTER ALL...
I THOUGHT HE WAS JUST GREEDY...
THIS SCHOOL WAS MY TOP CHOICE WHEN I WAS TAKING THE PLACEMENT EXAMS... BUT I DIDN'T APPLY.
SINCE I KNEW THERE WAS A DORMITORY...
WHAT? WHY DIDN'T YOU JUST APPLY?
YEAH! IF THEY ALLOWED YOU TO TRANSFER HERE YOU MUST HAVE BEEN QUALIFIED.

SAYAKA FOUND OUT I WAS TRYING TO GET INTO THE DORMS, AND SHE WAS FURIOUS.

SHE PERSUADED MY UNCLE TO STOP ME, AND I COULDN'T SAY NO WITH HIM BEGGING ME TO STAY...

SIGH

SO THAT'S HOW I ENDED UP WITH YOU GUYS. PRETTY CRAZY.

KOUNO...

SO...

WERE YOU ABLE TO WORK THINGS OUT WITH HER?

WORK THINGS OUT...?
HAH HAH
KISSSSSSSS

UNG
I JUST REMEMBERED...
THE CONVERSATION WASN'T GOING ANYWHERE SO I CLEVERLY SUGGESTED THAT SHE PLEASE LEAVE FOR THE TIME BEING.

CLEVER, HUH?!

HOLD ON!

WH... WHAT HAPPENED...?

IT MUST HAVE BEEN CLEVER IF SHE RAN HOME CRYING LIKE THAT.

RAN HOME CRYING...?

THAT WASN'T CLEVER AT ALL! ANY NORMAL GUY WOULD HAVE TO BE DRUNK TO KISS ANOTHER GUY!!

BE GLAD IT WAS A BEAUTIFUL MAN LIKE ME AND NOT SOMEONE WEIRD. YOU SHOULD FEEL LUCKY!

THIS...

A LOVER'S QUARREL...?

DID...

DID YOU GUYS KISS?

BEAUTIFUL OR NOT... A MAN'S MOUTH IS STILL A *MAN'S MOUTH*.
HNFF

THEN WHAT?! ARE YOU SAYING MY FACE IS NO BETTER THAN THAT OF SOMEONE WHO LOOKS LIKE A GORILLA, OR A FISH, OR A POTATO?

LIKE THIS

OR THIS

OR LIKE THIS?!

HAVE YOU NO SENSE OF BEAUTY?!

AND YOU CALL YOURSELF A PRINCESS?!

BETWEEN *ME,* WHO HAS GRACE, ELEGANCE, AND CLEANLI-NESS...

むーん NNF

AND A GUY YOU MIGHT FIND IN THE JUDO CLUB... RUGGED, SMELLY AND UNCOOL... WHO WOULD YOU RATHER KISS?

UH...

THE GUYS IN THE JUDO CLUB ARE KINDA-- BUT THEN, CONSIDERING SHIHOUDANI'S PERSONALITY, HE'S NOT SO GREAT, EITHER...
NNNG...
BROOD
BROOD
THERE'S NO WAY OUT OF IT. YOU HAVE TO PICK ONE.
IT DOESN'T MATTER WHO IT IS! I DON'T WANT TO KISS ANYONE BUT MY GIRLFRIEND!!
GRAAAAHHH
GREAT. THAT DOESN'T TELL US ANYTHING.
YOU'RE NO HELP!
GAAAH
GAAAH
WAAAH
BUT MY GIRLFRIEND IS HOT!
GAAAH
NO ONE ASKED YOU!
WAAAH
H-HEY, CALM DOWN YOU GUYS...
ALL RIGHT, WHAT ABOUT *YOU*, SAKAMOTO?
WHIP

ER...
AH...
UM...
UH...

ガイヤッ
GA-CHAK
パタン…
BATAM
HEY. YOU'RE BACK LATE.
YEAH...

I GOT THIRSTY SO I WENT OUT TO GET SOMETHING TO DRINK. HERE.
OH, YOU GOT ONE FOR ME? THANKS.
DON'T WORRY ABOUT IT. IT'S FREE ANYWAY.
FOR PRINCESSES.
I KNOW, BUT STILL... THANKS.
PSHT
SO...
DID YOU FIGURE OUT WHAT TO DO ABOUT YOUR SISTER?

I HAVE NO CLUE. NO MATTER WHAT I SAY, SHE'S JUST GOING TO RESPOND AS THOUGH SHE NEVER HEARD ME AT ALL. I'M AT A LOSS.
MAYBE SHE DOES IT UNCONSCIOUSLY, BUT SHE SEEMS TO ONLY HEAR WHAT SHE WANTS TO HEAR.
WHINING SO SHE CAN GET WHAT SHE WANTS... SHE'S LIKE A BABY! SHE'S A BIG LUMP OF SELFISHNESS!
SHE'S SO TERRIBLE IT MAKES ME SICK!
DNK
SHE DOESN'T WANT TO HEAR ANYTHING THAT ISN'T BENEFICIAL TO HER.
YUUJIROU ...

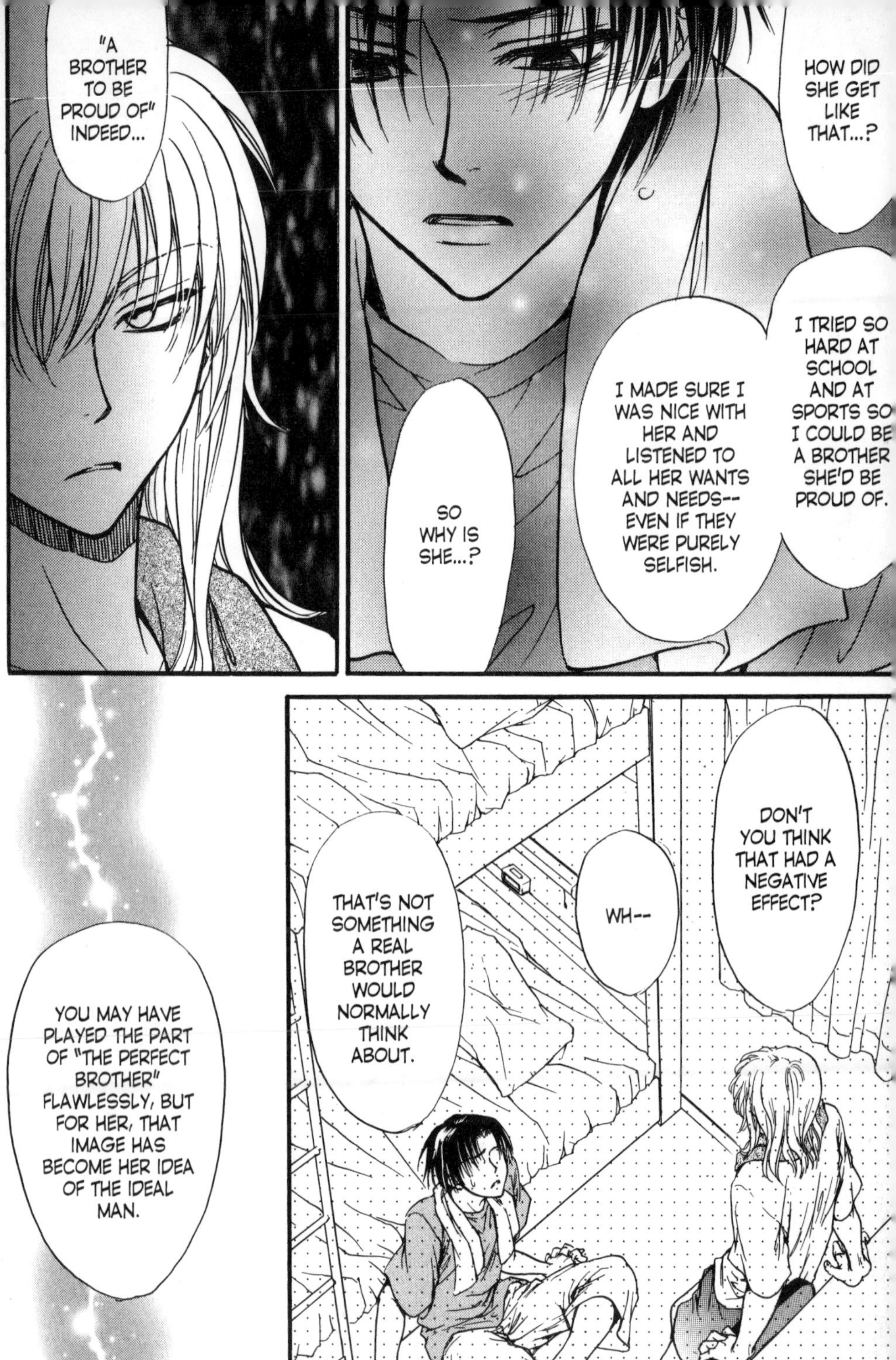

HOW DID SHE GET LIKE THAT...?

I TRIED SO HARD AT SCHOOL AND AT SPORTS SO I COULD BE A BROTHER SHE'D BE PROUD OF.

I MADE SURE I WAS NICE WITH HER AND LISTENED TO ALL HER WANTS AND NEEDS-- EVEN IF THEY WERE PURELY SELFISH.

SO WHY IS SHE...?

"A BROTHER TO BE PROUD OF" INDEED...

DON'T YOU THINK THAT HAD A NEGATIVE EFFECT?
WH--
THAT'S NOT SOMETHING A REAL BROTHER WOULD NORMALLY THINK ABOUT.

YOU MAY HAVE PLAYED THE PART OF "THE PERFECT BROTHER" FLAWLESSLY, BUT FOR HER, THAT IMAGE HAS BECOME HER IDEA OF THE IDEAL MAN.

SOMEONE WHO'S ATTRACTIVE, DEPENDABLE, HAS A GOOD PERSONALITY AND IS NICE TO HER...
IT'S REASONABLE TO THINK THAT SHE WOULD MISTAKE ALL OF THAT FOR AFFECTION.
NO WAY...
WAS I... WAS I WRONG...?
NO! SHE'S TRYING TO GET WHAT SHE CAN'T HAVE! *SHE'S* THE ONE WHO'S *WRONG!*
BUT IF ANYTHING IS YOUR FAULT IN THIS...
IT'S THAT YOU WON'T COME OUT AND TELL HER HOW YOU HONESTLY FEEL.

I TOLD HER THAT I DIDN'T THINK OF HER AS ANYTHING BUT MY--
SHE KNOWS YOU THINK OF HER AS A SISTER, BUT WHAT ABOUT YOUR FEELINGS?
IF YOU DON'T EVER TELL HER HOW YOU HONESTLY FEEL, THEN SHE WON'T THINK YOU'RE GENUINELY REJECTING HER, AND NOTHING WILL CHANGE.

HOW I HONESTLY FEEL...?

I CAN'T STAND HER...

I DON'T LIKE HOW HER PARENTS HAVE SPOILED HER ROTTEN.

IT PISSES ME OFF WHEN SHE ACTS SELFISH, AND THEN DEMANDS THINGS OF ME AS IF IT'S HER RIGHT.

I PUT UP WITH IT BECAUSE SHE'S MY UNCLE'S DAUGHTER, BUT IF THAT WASN'T THE CASE, I WOULDN'T EVEN GO NEAR HER.

BUT I CAN'T TELL SAYAKA SOMETHING LIKE THAT.

HER PARENTS ARE MY GUARDIANS...

AH, I SEE.
I WAS WONDERING WHY YOU GAVE HER SUCH A ROUNDABOUT REASON.
YUUJIROU ...
BUT YOU HAVE TO TELL HER.
SHE KNOWS YOU LOVE HER AS A SISTER, SO SHE THINKS IF SHE KEEPS PUSHING YOU, SOMETHING MORE MIGHT COME OF IT. THAT'S PROBABLY WHY SHE'S TRYING SO DESPERATELY.
SLUMP
DON'T MAKE ME SAY THESE THINGS...
IT'S JUST SHAMEFUL...
MY AUNT AND UNCLE ACTUALLY WANT ME TO BE WITH HER...
THEY KNOW ME WELL, AND THEY WANT THEIR DAUGHTER TO BE HAPPY AND NOT SO TORN ABOUT IT ALL...
THAT'S WHY... I'M SCARED THAT IF I TELL SAYAKA WHAT I THINK ABOUT HER, IT MIGHT RUIN THINGS BETWEEN ME AND THEM...

LOSING THAT PROTECTIVE WING IS LIKE FALLING STRAIGHT INTO A BLACK HOLE. JUST THE THOUGHT OF IT SCARES THE HELL OUT OF ME.

I'D FEEL BLIND AND FROZEN WITH FEAR, NOT KNOWING WHAT TO DO OR WHAT WOULD HAPPEN TO ME.

THAT'S HOW I FELT WHEN MY PARENTS DIED A LONG TIME AGO.

EXCEPT ...
THAT WAS WHEN YOU WERE ONLY A CHILD, RIGHT? YOU DIDN'T KNOW HOW TO SURVIVE ON YOUR OWN.

BUT YOU'RE OLD ENOUGH NOW. YOU'RE WISER, AND YOU KNOW WHAT YOU NEED TO DO.
AND YOU'VE GOT STURDY HANDS AND FEET TO GET A JOB AND SUPPORT YOURSELF.
AH...

I GUESS... YOU'RE RIGHT... IT'S A DIFFERENT SITUATION THAN BEFORE...

I'M NOT...

...JUST A KID ANYMORE.

ぎゅっ
CLENCH
THE POWER TO LIVE...
ふっ...
FSHH
...TO SHAPE MY FUTURE...
...IS IN MY HANDS NOW.
MAYBE...
I'M NOT QUITE READY TO CUT MYSELF LOOSE COMPLETELY...
BUT BECAUSE OF YOU, I FEEL A LOT BETTER ABOUT THINGS. THANKS, YUUJIROU.

SO,

FOR NOW, DO YOU THINK YOU'LL BE ABLE TO DEAL WITH YOUR SISTER THE NEXT TIME SHE COMES?

HHUP!

HMM, WE'LL SEE... I DON'T THINK IT'LL BE ALL THAT EASY, THOUGH.

BUT I DO FEEL LIKE I'LL AT LEAST BE READY FOR IT NEXT TIME.

WELL, THE ONLY REASON I CAN TOSS OUT IDEAS IS BECAUSE I DON'T HAVE TO DEAL WITH IT MYSELF.

IF THAT GOT DUMPED ON ME ALL OF A SUDDEN, I WOULD BE COMPLETELY LOST.

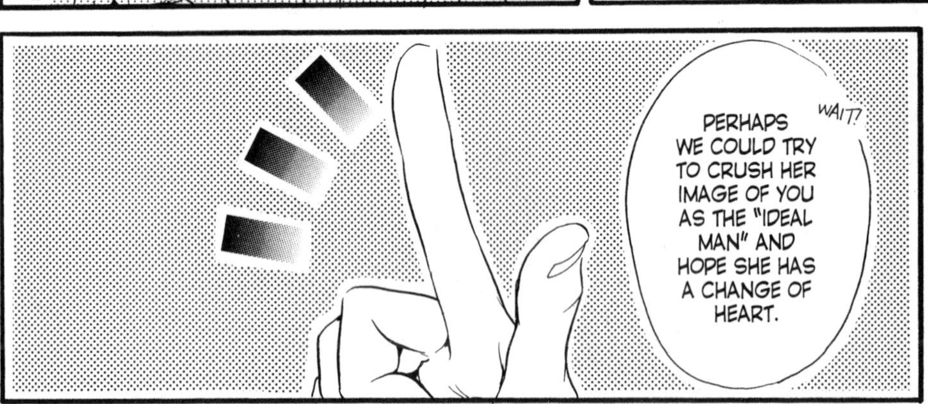
WAIT!
PERHAPS WE COULD TRY TO CRUSH HER IMAGE OF YOU AS THE "IDEAL MAN" AND HOPE SHE HAS A CHANGE OF HEART.

HEY, I THINK THAT MIGHT ACTUALLY BE REALLY EFFECTIVE!
YEAH!
HUH?
BY DOING *THAT?*

SHE RAN OFF WHEN WE MADE HER THINK YOU WERE GAY, DIDN'T SHE? AND SHE WAS ALREADY PUT OFF BY THE PRINCESS OUTFIT.

GIRLS TODAY WHO CALL ABOUT ANYTHING "CUTE" WOULD JUST LAUGH AT SOMETHING LIKE THAT.

BUT THE WAY SHE REACTED PROBABLY MEANS SHE'S FIXATED ON THE IDEA THAT YOU, HER "IDEAL MAN", ARE A PERFECT HUMAN BEING, WHO WOULD NEVER DO ANYTHING STRANGE LIKE THAT.

THAT'S RIGHT.

BUT WHAT CAN I DO...?

I WORKED HARD TO BECOME THE "PERFECT BROTHER", BUT I'VE BEEN LIKE THAT FOR SO LONG THAT IT'S KIND OF WHO I AM.

SHOW HER YOUR TRUE NATURE?

AND WHAT'S MY TRUE NATURE?

YOUR COLD, BLACK HEART.

AND FOR THE FINAL BLOW, SHOW HER YOU'RE A DELINQUENT.

A DELIN-QUENT?

YOU MEAN DYE MY HAIR AND ALTER MY UNIFORM? AND THEN TAKE UP SMOKING AND RIDE AROUND ON A REALLY LOUD MOTORCYCLE?

SOMEHOW THAT SEEMS LIKE A WASTE OF TIME. AND IT TAKES MONEY. AND IT'S BAD FOR MY HEALTH.

I GUESS YOUR HEART ISN'T SO BLACK, THEN.

NO WAY.

NOT IF THOSE ARE YOUR REASONS ...

WELL, YOU'LL JUST HAVE TO THINK ABOUT WHAT TO DO NEXT TIME SHE COMES.

NNNG...

DIIING DOOOONG
DIIING DOOOONG
DIIING DOOOONG
DIIING DOOOONG
WELL, THEN, EVERYONE ...
I HOPE THAT ALL OF YOU ENDEAVOR TO HAVE A SAFE AND ENJOYABLE VACATION. THAT'S ALL FOR TODAY.
CLASS DISMISSED.
WOOO!
STAND
STAND
STAND
STAND
IT'S OVER! VACATION TIME!
LET'S GO HOME!
WHAT ARE YOU DOING TODAY?
LET'S GO!

VACATION TIME...
ふー…
SIGH
WITH OUR WORK BEING PRINCESSES, IT'S HARD TO SAY WE LIVE A RELAXED LIFE-STYLE.
MAYBE. BUT THE ATHLETIC CLUBS WE HAVE TO CHEER FOR ARE FORCED TO BE AT PRACTICE EVERY DAY, SO THEY HAVE IT WORSE THAN WE DO.
THE LEAST WE HAVE TO DO IS GO TO TOURNA-MENTS.
FORCED ...?
I SEE...
I THINK I'M GOING TO HAVE MUCH MORE FREEDOM DURING THIS VACATION THAN I'VE EVER HAD.

PRIN-CESSES!
WE MAY SEE YOU ON CAMPUS, BUT SADLY IT WILL BE LONG BEFORE WE GAZE UPON YOU ONCE MORE.
KUH...
STAND
PLEASE! GRACE ME ONCE MORE WITH YOUR SMILES, SO THAT I MAY ETCH THEM IN MY MIND'S EYE TO REMEMBER THEM!!
PLEASE, BEFORE WE GO!
STAND
STAND
ME TOO, PLEASE!
AND ME!!
PLEASE!
STAND
CHUCKLE
THE PRINCESS SMILE.
STAY HEALTHY EVERYONE. AND PLEASE BE SAFE.
LET'S ALL HAVE A FUN VACATION!
SMILE

うおおーっ
OOOHHHHH!
THANK YOU FOR THE WONDERFUL PARTING GIFT, PRINCESSES!!
BYE!
YOU'RE THE BEST!
THANKS, PRINCESSES!
SEE YOU!
'TIS A SHAME WE SHALL NOT MEET AGAIN FOR SOME TIME, BUT NOW I MAY RETURN HOME WITH A CALM HEART.
THEY CAN LOOK AT ALL THE GIRLS THEY WANT WHEN THEY GO HOME... WHY DO THEY GO OUT OF THEIR WAY TO SEE FAKES LIKE US?
BECAUSE WE'RE THEY'RE BACK-UPS. IF THEY MEET A GIRL AND GET SHOT DOWN, THEY'LL STILL HAVE US WHEN THEY COME BACK.
SO WEIRD...

YOU TWO ALWAYS HAVE A BIG AUDIENCE FOR YOUR SEND-OFFS.

AH, SAKAMOTO.

I DON'T THINK YOU'RE IN A POSITION TO COMMENT, SINCE WHEREVER *YOU* GO ALL THE PEOPLE BOW TO YOU.

ER

YEAH, SERIOUSLY.

SO ARE YOU TWO HEADING OFF ALREADY?

YEAH... WELL, TO THE DORMS AT LEAST. WE'RE NOT GOING HOME.

AREN'T YOU GOING HOME YET?
YOU'VE GOT YOUR NOTES...
YES. I'M ON MY WAY TO A STUDENT COUNCIL MEETING.
WOW, THAT'S ROUGH...
THEY MUST REALLY LIKE YOU OVER THERE, EH, SAKAMOTO-*SAMA*?

LIKE I SAID BEFORE, YOU SHOULD COME OVER TO MY HOUSE SOMETIME. JUST GIVE ME A CALL.
YEAH, WE WILL! TAKE IT EASY!
WELL,
LIFT
BETTER GET GOING.
HA HA
BACK TO THE DORMS.
BACK TO THE DORMS.

WOULD YA LOOK AT THAT? LEAVING RIGHT AWAY, JUST AS WE THOUGHT.

COULDN'T EVEN WAIT UNTIL THE FIRST DAY OF VACATION. THE ASSEMBLY JUST FINISHED AND NOW HE'S LEAVING.

HMMMM

UGHH

HOW COLD! YOU'RE JUST GOING TO THROW US ASIDE AND GO HOME TO YOUR WIFE?

AHHH

WAS IT ALL A LIE? DO WE MEAN NOTHING TO YOU? HOW CRUEL!!

SOB SOB

COLLAPSE

NO... I KNOW THE REAL REASON... WE'VE NOTHING BUT A SHALLOW MEANINGLESS RELATIONSHIP...
YES. AFTER ALL, THE CONNECTION BETWEEN US IS AS THIN AS PAPER...
CHUCKLE
...YOU GUYS...
KNOCK IT OFF WITH THE CREEPY ACT!!
FINE. IF YOU PREFER THE REGULAR WAY...
JUST AS I THOUGHT, YOUR FRIENDS ARE WORTH NOTHING COMPARED TO YOUR GIRLFRIEND.
UN-GRATEFUL JERK.
ARGH
UNGRATEFUL, HUH?! I'M WITH YOU GUYS EVERY DAY!
IF THERE'S ANYONE I'VE BEEN UNGRATEFUL TO IT'S MY GIRLFRIEND! I HARDLY EVER GET TO SEE HER!!

IS THERE SOMETHING WRONG WITH GOING HOME EARLY TO MAKE UP FOR LOST TIME?!
WELL?
NO, THERE'S NOTHING WRONG WITH IT.
I'M JEALOUS, ACTUALLY.
IT'S GREAT THAT YOU LOVE HER SO MUCH.
SAME HERE.
えっ...
UH
TH... THEN WHY ARE YOU GUYS PICKING ON ME ABOUT IT?
BECAUSE! YOU WERE SO EXCITED THAT YOU'D GET TO SEE YOUR GIRLFRIEND.
WE HAD TO MAKE SURE WE DROVE THE NAIL IN BEFORE YOU GET WRAPPED UP IN YOUR GIRLFRIEND OVER VACATION AND DITCH OUT ON BEING A PRINCESS.
DON'T TELL ME YOU HAVEN'T THOUGHT ABOUT IT.
う...
UGH...
YOU'RE RIGHT... I HAVE...

HERE'S A QUESTION FOR YOU, MIKOTO.
LET'S SAY YOU HAVE PLANS WITH YOUR GIRLFRIEND, BUT AN EVENT FOR PRINCESSES IS SCHEDULED TO HAPPEN AT THE SAME TIME. WHAT WOULD YOU DO?
UH...
WHAT WOULD I DO? WELL I NEVER WANTED TO BE A PRINCESS IN THE FIRST PLACE, AND OF COURSE I'D WANT TO SPEND TIME WITH MY GIRLFRIEND... BUT I'M OBLIGATED TO BE A PRINCESS, SO THAT TAKES PRIORITY... UMM...
PAP
FPA
YOU SHOULDN'T HAVE TO THINK ABOUT IT!
YOU SHOULD ANSWER "PRINCESS" RIGHT AWAY!

DON'T HIT ME WITH YOUR DIRTY SLIPPERS!!
AND THEY HURT!
GRAB
がはっ
CALM DOWN. AT LEAST WE DIDN'T HIT YOU WITH BATHROOM SLIPPERS.
I SMELL TREACHERY. IF HIS GIRLFRIEND IS A BIGGER PRIORITY, HE MIGHT JUST DITCH OUT ON HIS WORK. WHAT SHOULD WE DO?
HMM...
IF HIS GIRLFRIEND IS THAT IMPORTANT TO HIM, THEN THAT MUST BE HIS WEAKNESS.
GRIN
ニヤ
MIKOTO!
FLINCH
ビクッ
IF YOU SKIP OUT ON YOUR DUTIES AS A PRINCESS EVEN ONCE...

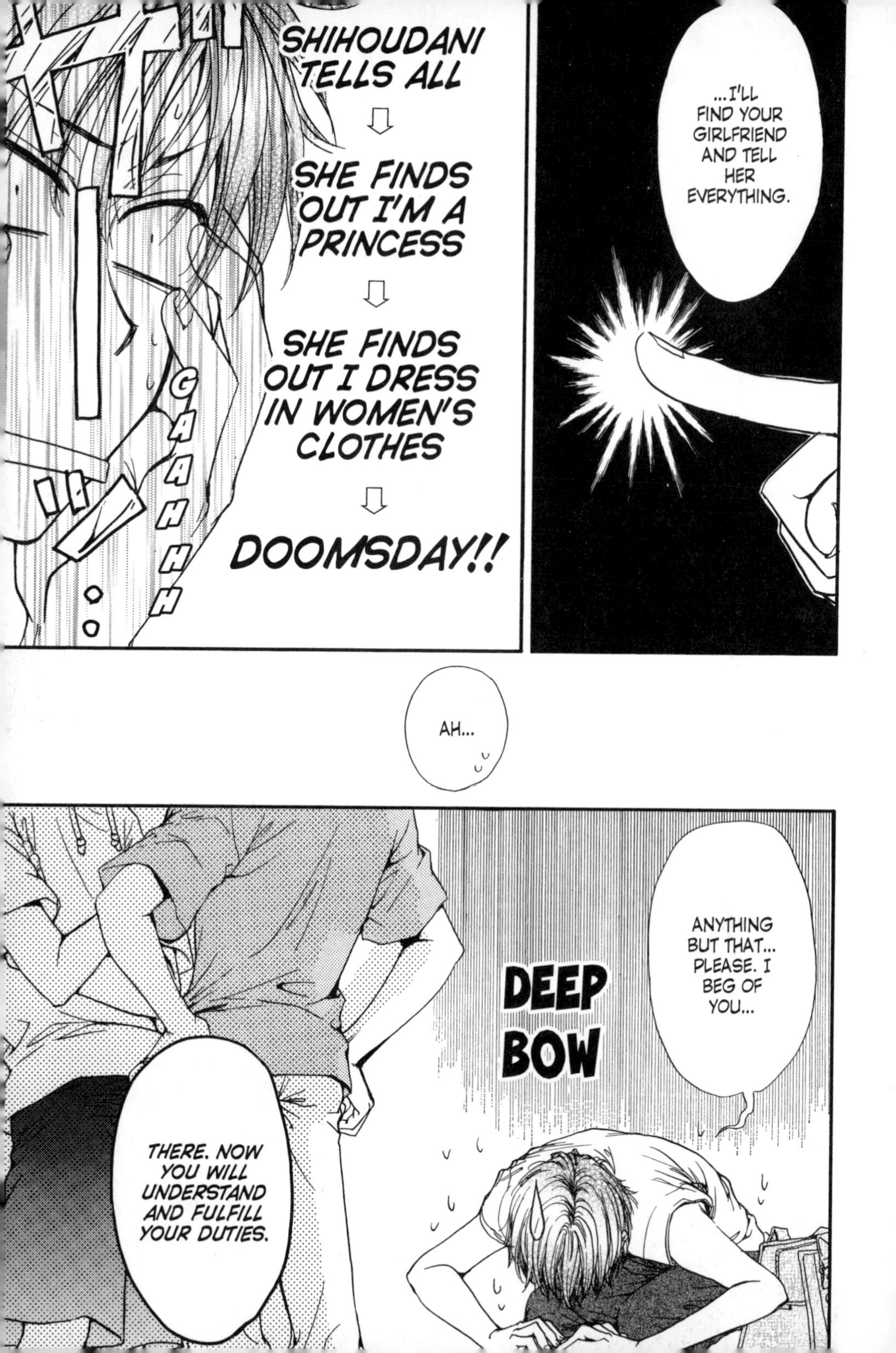

AH...

ANYTHING BUT THAT... PLEASE. I BEG OF YOU...

DEEP BOW

THERE. NOW YOU WILL UNDERSTAND AND FULFILL YOUR DUTIES.

I...
BUT I THOUGHT IT WOULD BE COLD-HEARTED IF I JUST LEFT, SO I MADE SURE TO SAY SOMETHING. AND YOU MADE FUN OF ME, JUST AS I THOUGHT YOU WOULD...
I THOUGHT ABOUT JUST GOING HOME WITHOUT SAYING ANYTHING... I KNEW IF I SAID GOODBYE YOU TWO WOULD MAKE FUN OF ME...
I KNEW I SHOULD'VE JUST LEFT!
RISE
DAMNIT!
YOU MORON. YOU KNOW IF YOU LEFT WITHOUT SAYING ANYTHING, WE'D MAKE FUN OF YOU AS SOON AS YOU GOT BACK, ANYWAY.
THEN YOU'D BE MIKOTO THE COLD-HEARTED.
SHOULDA SEEN THAT COMING.
SHIHOUDANI... AND... AND KOUNO...
YOU'RE BOTH...
SHAKE
SHAKE

JEEEERKS!!
DASH
DON'T FORGET YOU'RE A PRINCESS!
SO HE'S GONE, THEN...
IT'LL BE LONELY WITHOUT HIM AROUND...
OR QUIET, AT LEAST...
THERE AREN'T MANY PEOPLE THAT ARE AS FUN TO MESS WITH AS HE IS.
I DON'T THINK MIKOTO IS NOTICING YOUR SPECIAL AFFECTION.
I HOPE HE NEVER DOES. IF HE DID, HE WOULDN'T BE FUN TO MESS WITH ANYMORE.
...I KIND OF FEEL SORRY FOR HIM...
PATAM

BZZZZ
BZZ
BZZ
MEEEEE...
MEEEN...

PTAK

IT'S SO HOT!!

IT'S THIS HOT AND THEY'RE NOT GOING TO LET US USE THE AIR CONDITIONER?! ARE THEY INSANE? DID THEY FORGET THERE ARE STILL STUDENTS LIVING HERE?!

IT'S SO HOT I CAN'T EVEN *STUDY!!*

THEY CAN'T REALLY LEAVE THE AIR CONDITIONING ON FOR ONLY A HANDFUL OF STUDENTS. THE ELECTRIC BILL WOULD BE RIDICULOUS.

IT'S HOTTER THAN THE SUN!!
STOP TALKING ABOUT IT SO MUCH. IT JUST MAKES IT FEEL HOTTER.

I KNOW, I KNOW.
BUT STILL...

WANT TO GO TO THE STORE?
IT'S COOL IN THERE.
BUT WE CAN'T JUST SIT IN THERE FOR VERY LONG...
WHAT'S A NICE COOL PLACE WE CAN RELAX IN...?
HMM...
A PLACE WE COULD STUDY...
HMM...

OH!

THE LIBRARY! THE CITY LIBRARY IS ONLY A SEVEN- OR EIGHT-MINUTE WALK FROM HERE.

IT'S AIR CONDITIONED AND WE CAN STAY THERE AS LONG AS WE WANT!

OH, YEAH.

AND IT'S QUIET IN THERE, SO WE CAN MAKE SOME HEADWAY ON THIS HOMEWORK...

EXACTLY!

LET'S LEAVE RIGHT NOW, THEN!
OKAY!

MEEEEE
BZZZZZ

ARE WE THERE YET? IT'S SO HOT...
IT SHOULD BE RIGHT HERE.
THERE IT IS! I SEE IT!

HAAA
はー…
AHH, IT'S SO COOL.
AH!
LOOK! VENDING MA-CHINES!
WHY DON'T WE REPLENISH OURSELVES FIRST?
FINE BY ME. I'M THIRSTY!

HEY TOHRU, DO YOU KNOW HOW TO DO THIS ONE?
THIS ONE HERE.
HM? THE SECOND ONE?
HMM...
OH, THAT FORMULA?
BEATS ME... I DON'T UNDERSTAND THIS STUFF AT ALL...
IF SAKAMOTO WERE HERE, HE COULD TELL US.
DIDN'T SAKAMOTO INVITE US TO HIS HOUSE?
LET'S GO HANG OUT AT HIS PLACE AND ASK FOR HELP WHILE WE'RE THERE.
AH, THEN HE CAN SHOW US HOW TO DO SOME OF THE HARDER ONES, AND WE CAN HAVE HIM CHECK OUR WORK.
WAIT!

HOW OLD ARE YOU?
WE'RE IN OUR FIRST YEAR OF COLLEGE.
HEY, WANT US TO HELP YOU STUDY?
WHAT?!
WHOA, WHOA...
WE NOTICED YOU TWO A LITTLE BIT AGO, AND WE THOUGHT YOU WERE BOTH CUTE.
SO WE CAME TO SAY HI.
HANG ON. WE'RE NOT WEARING PRINCESS COSTUMES. HOW COULD THEY MISTAKE US FOR GIRLS?!
HOW ABOUT GOING OUT FOR COFFEE WITH US?
AND WE'RE NOT WEARING PARTICULARLY FEMININE CLOTHES. WHERE ARE THEY LOOKING?!
WE DON'T HAVE BOOBS!
HOW ABOUT IT, GIRLS?
DID THEY MEAN US?!
AND WHO PICKS UP ON GIRLS IN THE LIBRARY?!
ガタ
STAND
ガタッ
STAND

HOW OLD ARE YOU?
WE'RE IN OUR FIRST YEAR OF COLLEGE.
HEY, WANT US TO HELP YOU STUDY?
WHAT?!
WHOA, WHOA...
WE NOTICED YOU TWO A LITTLE BIT AGO, AND WE THOUGHT YOU WERE BOTH CUTE.
SO WE CAME TO SAY HI.
HANG ON. WE'RE NOT WEARING PRINCESS COSTUMES. HOW COULD THEY MISTAKE US FOR GIRLS?!
HOW ABOUT GOING OUT FOR COFFEE WITH US?
AND WE'RE NOT WEARING PARTICULARLY FEMININE CLOTHES. WHERE ARE THEY LOOKING?!
WE DON'T HAVE BOOBS!
HOW ABOUT IT, GIRLS?
DID THEY MEAN US?!
AND WHO PICKS UP ON GIRLS IN THE LIBRARY?!
STAND
STAND

UMM...
WELL... HAPPY BIRTHDAY...
THANKS.

AND... YOU WANT ME TO GET YOU SOMETHING?
IS THAT WHY YOU TOLD ME?

NOT REALLY.
I DON'T WANT A WHOLE ONE OR ANYTHING, BUT IT WOULD BE NICE TO HAVE A BIT OF CAKE.

ALL RIGHT... I'LL GO TO THE STORE TOMORROW AND GET YOU A CUPCAKE...

SO YOU DO WANT SOME-THING.

DON'T BE A CHEAPSKATE. GO GET ONE FROM A BAKERY.

BE GLAD I'M GETTING YOU ANYTHING...
HEY GIIIRLS!

SO WHEN SHOULD WE GO THERE?
GOING DURING THE OBON FESTIVAL PROBABLY ISN'T TOO GREAT.
AND THERE'S THE POSSIBILITY THAT HIS FAMILY MIGHT GO ON VACATION.
THOUGH HE NEVER MENTIONED IT.

WE COULD TRY TO SQUEEZE IT IN THIS MONTH, OR THE BEGINNING OF THE NEXT...
OR THE END OF NEXT MONTH, BUT THAT'S A BUSY TIME...
SO MAYBE WE SHOULD TRY TO GO THIS MONTH AFTER ALL...
THIS IS UNRELATED, BUT DID YOU KNOW MY BIRTHDAY IS TOMORROW?

HUH?
WHAT?
YOUR BIRTHDAY?
TOMORROW?

HEY TOHRU, DO YOU KNOW HOW TO DO THIS ONE?
THIS ONE HERE.
HM? THE SECOND ONE?
HMM...
OH, THAT FORMULA?
BEATS ME... I DON'T UNDERSTAND THIS STUFF AT ALL...
IF SAKAMOTO WERE HERE, HE COULD TELL US.
WAIT!
DIDN'T SAKAMOTO INVITE US TO HIS HOUSE?
LET'S GO HANG OUT AT HIS PLACE AND ASK FOR HELP WHILE WE'RE THERE.
AH, THEN HE CAN SHOW US HOW TO DO SOME OF THE HARDER ONES, AND WE CAN HAVE HIM CHECK OUR WORK.

にっこり…
SMILE
AHHHY♥
THEY'RE SO CUTE!!
YOU'LL GO?
BONK
ズッ
WE'RE BOTH GUYS, YOU IDIOTS!!
KA-
HM?
HUH?

STOMP
STOMP
STOMP

HOW COULD THEY MISTAKE US FOR GIRLS?! THEY MUST NEED GLASSES!!

AND IF YOU WANT TO PICK UP CHICKS, DO IT SOMEWHERE BESIDES THE DAMN LIBRARY!!

WELL THE POINT IS, THOSE COLLEGE GUYS ARE THE ONES TO BLAME HERE!
RIGHT! IT'S NOT ***OUR*** FAULT!
NO WAY!
GAH! NOW I'M ALL SWEATY FROM GETTING WORKED UP.
THIS IS ALL THEIR FAULT.
SERIOUSLY.
I'M TAKING A SHOWER AS ***SOON*** AS WE GET BACK.

SHIHOUDANI-KUN OF CLASS 1-D, YOU HAVE A PHONE CALL FROM HOME. PLEASE PICK UP THE PHONE LINE NEAREST YOU.
REPEAT.
THERE IS A CALL FOR SHIHOUDANI-KUN OF CLASS 1-D. PLEASE FIND THE PHONE NEAREST YOU.
HUH?
A CALL FROM HOME...?
YUUJIROU?

ガチャッ
GA-CHAK
はっ
AH
どさっ
PLOP
SHHHT
パターン
BATAM
ばさっ
FWFF

PLOP

YUUJI-ROU...

WAS THAT A CALL FROM HOME? IS EVERYTHING OKAY...?

EVERY-THING'S FINE.
THEY JUST ASKED IF I WOULD BE GOING HOME FOR MY BIRTHDAY.
I TOLD THEM I'D FEEL BAD LEAVING MY ROOMMATE ALL BY HIMSELF, SO I'M STAYING HERE.
YOU'D GET LONELY WITH NO ONE ELSE AROUND, RIGHT?
...YUUJI-ROU...
ARE YOU SURE YOU'RE OKAY WITH THAT...?
...
...

むくっ
RISE
TOHRU.
HM?

LET'S GO PICK UP ON GIRLS TOMORROW.
...
HUH?

WELL, IT'S MY BIRTHDAY, AND IT'LL BE DULL IF IT'S JUST YOU AND ME.
LET'S FIND SOME GIRLS AND GO WILD!
BUT... WHAT ABOUT YOUR...?

WHAT? DON'T WANT TO?

SURE...

I'LL GO WITH YOU.

...THANKS...

BUSTLE
BUSTLE
BUSTLE
大黒屋

TOHRU, DO YOU KNOW WHAT THEY CALL IT WHEN TWO PEOPLE GO SOMEWHERE TOGETHER? THEY CALL IT A DATE.

YOU REALLY WANT TO PICK UP GIRLS?
IF YOU JUST WANT TO HAVE FUN, THERE ARE PLENTY OF PLACES WE CAN GO OURSELVES.

SHOULD WE GO TO KARAOKE? OR AN ARCADE?

LET'S FIND SOME GIRLS!
GOOD.

FIRST, WE'LL HAVE TO SEARCH AROUND A LITTLE.
WHILE WE'RE AT IT, WHAT TYPE OF GIRLS DO YOU LIKE?
UMM...
IF I HAD TO CALL IT SOMETHING, I GUESS I'D SAY THE SOOTHING TYPE.

SO WHAT'S *YOUR* TYPE, THEN?
WELL... THERE'S ONE THING THAT THEY ABSOLUTELY HAVE TO HAVE...
BIG TITS.
THOUGH THEY CAN'T BE SO BIG THEY LOOK LIKE EGGPLANTS.
BOING BOING
THEY HAVE TO BE PERFECT BREASTS THAT I CAN NESTLE MY FACE BETWEEN.
AND THEN, THE AREOLA HAS TO MATCH THE NIPPLE PERFECTLY.
THE PERFECT BREAST WOULD HAVE ONE ABOUT THE SIZE OF A GRAPE, WITH A SOFT RING AROUND IT CLEARLY DEFINED BY ITS SLIGHTLY LIGHTER COLOR. AND IN THE MIDDLE THERE WOULD BE A FIRM, PERKY NIPPLE...
CD-SIZED
OKAY, STOP!

WHAT I ASKED WAS WHAT TYPE OF *GIRL* YOU LIKED, NOT WHAT TYPE OF ***CHEST***.
OH... THAT'S RIGHT.

SORRY. WHEN BREASTS CAME UP, I GOT CARRIED AWAY.

IT'S OKAY. AS A FELLOW GUY, I FEEL THE SAME WAY.

BUT WE SHOULDN'T BE TALKING ABOUT IT OUT ON THE STREET AROUND SO MANY PEOPLE.

IT ALSO FEELS A LITTLE WEIRD HEARING YOU TALK ABOUT BREASTS, CONSIDERING HOW YOU LOOK... SCARY, ACTUALLY.

WHAT? IT DOESN'T MATTER WHAT I LOOK LIKE. I'M A GUY! WOULDN'T IT BE WEIRDER IF I HAD NO INTEREST IN THE FEMALE BODY AT ALL?

NO, I'M NOT SAYING IT'S WEIRD TO LIKE THEM. I'M JUST SAYING THE WAY YOU LOOK AND WHAT YOU'RE SAYING DON'T MATCH.

IMAGINE IF MIKOTO WAS STARTED TALKING DIRTY. WOULDN'T THAT LOOK WEIRD?

ニヤニヤ
SNICKER SNICKER
MIKOTO TALKING DIRTY...
I LIKE THIN GIRLS, SO I LIKE 'EM WITH SMALL TITS. THAT FIT RIGHT IN MY HANDS.
AND THEIR ANKLES? IF THEY GOT TIGHT ANKLES, THEY'RE TIGHT IN OTHER PLACES TOO.
HEH HEH HEH
AHA HAHA HA...
もやん…
PONDER

THAT *IS* WEIRD. I MEAN, HE'S A GUY, SO IT MAKES SENSE, BUT... THAT GIVES ME THE ***CREEPS.***
WOOOW...
DOESN'T IT? IT'S THE SAME KIND OF THING WITH YOU.

IN ANY CASE, WE'RE LOOKING FOR THE SOOTHING TYPE AND THE BIG TITS TYPE.
HMM... DO THOSE TWO TYPES SHOW UP TOGETHER MUCH?
WE DON'T HAVE TO LIMIT IT TO THAT SPECIFIC PAIR. AS LONG AS WE CAN HAVE SOME FUN, THAT'S GOOD ENOUGH.

WELL, IF IT DOESN'T WORK OUT...
THEN WHAT?

WE'LL LOWER OUR STANDARDS.
OH MAN...

OH, HEY. WHAT ABOUT THOSE TWO OVER THERE?
HM? WHERE?
THOSE TWO GIRLS NEAR THE ENTRANCE.
NO GOOD. THEY'VE BEEN LOOKING AT THEIR WATCHES CONSTANTLY. PROBABLY WAITING FOR SOMEONE.
WOW, YOU'RE GOOD AT THIS...
YOU MUST DO THIS A LOT.

HOW ABOUT THOSE THREE GIRLS BY THE WINDOW BEHIND YOU?

STARE

NO GOOD. NOT A SINGLE ONE OF THEM HAS BIG TITS.

LOWER YOUR STANDARDS A *LITTLE*...

REJECTED

THEY'RE PRETTY CUTE, TOO...

GATAM
THEN LET'S GO, BEFORE IT'S TOO LATE!

!!
OH, ARE YOU TWO LEAVING ALREADY? DO YOU HAVE A MINUTE?

IS IT JUST THE TWO OF YOU?
OH, LOOK, AND ONLY TWO OF US.
WE WERE JUST THINKING OF GOING BOWLING.
ARE THEY...?
OH NO...

WOULD YOU TWO LIKE TO COME ALONG?
COME WITH US!
C'MON! COME!
WHAT IS IT LATELY?
AND THERE ARE SO MANY OTHER GIRLS HERE...
GUYS ARE HITTING ON US AGAIN!!

UGH, IF THESE GUYS HOLD ME UP ANY LONGER, THE GIRL WITH THE RACK WILL BE GONE.
GLANCE
TOTALLY-GONE
AHH! SHE'S LEFT!!
GAHHH
PRICKLE PRICKLE
SNNNAP
YU... YUUJIROU...
DO YOU NEED GLASSES, OR SOMETHING? OR ARE YOU JUST GAY? WE'RE ***GUYS***, ALL RIGHT? STOP HITTING ON US, YOU PERVERTS!!
ROCK

W... WHAT? YOU TWO ARE GUYS?! SHIT! YOU TRICKED US, DIDN'T YOU?!
DON'T WEAR SUCH MISLEADING CLOTHES THEN, YOU IDIOTS!!
YOU'RE THE ONES WHO MADE THE MISTAKE AND HIT ON US. DON'T ACT LIKE IT'S OUR FAULT!
WHAT?!
ばっ
LUNGE
CUT IT OUT, YUUJIROU!
C'MON, WE'RE GOING!
ぐいっ
YANK

STOMP
STOMP
STOMP
TCH...
SHIT...

YUUJI-ROU!
I SAID, CUT IT OUT!
AND DON'T FOLLOW US!
YEAH RIGHT! YOU THINK WE'RE GONNA LET HIM GET AWAY WITH THAT?!
FWIP
IF YOU FOLLOW US, IT JUST MEANS YOU'RE GAY!
FREEZE
GUH

WHAT WAS THAT BACK THERE? WHY'D YOU DO THAT...?

NORMALLY YOU WOULD'VE HANDLED IT LIKE IT WASN'T A BIG DEAL.

...SORRY...

...LET'S HEAD BACK.
THEN... I WANT TO TELL YOU ABOUT MY PAST...
...OKAY.

I LOST MY PARENTS IN AN ACCIDENT.
THEN I WAS TAKEN IN AND RAISED BY MY UNCLE.
I WOULDN'T SAY I'VE BEEN TREATED BADLY, BUT THINGS WERE AWKWARD... THAT'S WHY I CAME HERE.
I'VE ALWAYS THOUGHT OF MY UNCLE'S DAUGHTER AS MY LITTLE SISTER, BUT WHEN SHE FELL FOR ME AND HURT SOMEONE, THERE WASN'T ANY OTHER CHOICE.

I LOST MY PARENTS... I LOST MY HOME...
WHEN I THINK ABOUT IT, I REALLY THINK... "WOW, I'VE LED A PRETTY HARD LIFE..."

BUT THERE MAY BE OTHERS OUT THERE WHO ARE THE SAME AS ME... I GET THAT FEELING FROM HIM...

YUUJIROU...

WHAT...

WHAT IN THE WORLD...

...COULD YOU HAVE BEEN THROUGH?

WHEN HE GOT THAT PHONE CALL AFTER WE GOT BACK FROM THE LIBRARY...
YOU GO AHEAD, TOHRU. I'LL BE BACK IN A MINUTE.
OH, OKAY. SURE...
HELLO, MOTHER. IS SOME-THING WRONG?
HM? TOMOR-ROW?
I ALREADY TOLD YOU I HAVE PLANS ALL THROUGH VACATION, SO I CAN'T GO HOME.
YEAH, I KNOW... BUT HAVING MY FAMILY CELEBRATE MY BIRTHDAY AT THIS AGE WOULD BE EMBAR-RASSING, ANYWAY.
NO, REALLY... IT'S FINE.
DON'T WORRY ABOUT ME. I'M ALL RIGHT.
...HE WAS TALKING CASUALLY WITH WHAT SOUNDED LIKE HIS MOTHER...

IT DIDN'T SEEM LIKE HE WAS PUSHING HIMSELF...
BUT HE WAS SO OPPOSED TO GOING HOME, AND NOW HE'S BROODING OVER IT. THERE MUST BE SOMETHING SERIOUS GOING ON...
SOMETHING HARD FOR HIM TO TALK ABOUT...
IT'S PROBABLY NOTHING LIKE LOSING HIS PARENTS. THAT WAS DEFINITELY HIS MOM ON THE PHONE...
HE PROBABLY DIDN'T HAVE A RELATIVE FALL IN LOVE WITH HIM. EVEN IF HE DID, HE SEEMS LIKE HE COULD HANDLE IT WELL ENOUGH.
MAYBE NOT A RELATIVE, BUT SOMEONE ELSE FELL FOR HIM!
EVEN PUTTING ASIDE HIS PERSONALITY, HE'S PRETTY ATTRACTIVE. HE DID GET CHOSEN AS A PRINCESS, SO HE'S GOT GOOD LOOKS.
HE MIGHT BE ABLE TO TALK HIS WAY OUT OF THINGS, BUT IF THERE WAS SOMEONE STRONGER THAN HIM PHYSICALLY, THEN...
OH, NO...

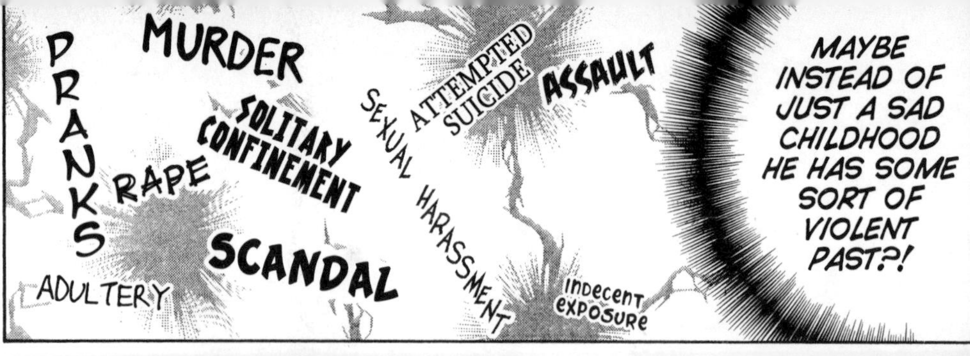

TOHRU...

どきいっ BA-BUMP

Y-YEAH?

ビクッ JUMP

IF I REALLY TELL YOU THESE THINGS, YOU MIGHT START TO ACT DIFFERENT TOWARDS ME...

SO THERE IS! THERE IS SOME SORT OF GHASTLY SOAP OPERA DRAMA!
WEIRD THING TO BRAG ABOUT
DON'T UNDERESTIMATE ME. I DON'T MEAN TO BRAG, BUT I HAD A PRETTY MISERABLE PAST, TOO.
NOW I'M IMMUNE!
THEN YOU SWEAR?
NO MATTER WHAT I TELL YOU, YOU WON'T TREAT ME DIFFER-ENTLY?
YEAH...
GULP
ごく…

ALL ALONG...
I'VE GROWN UP WITH ONLY MY MOTHER.
MY FATHER FELL ILL AND DIED BEFORE I WAS OLD ENOUGH TO BE AWARE...
BUT IT DIDN'T REALLY BOTHER ME.
BECAUSE I DIDN'T HAVE A FATHER TO START WITH, AND I NEVER KNEW WHAT HAVING ONE WAS LIKE. SO I NEVER REALLY *WANTED* ONE.
I ALWAYS FELT THAT I NEEDED TO HELP MY MOTHER OUT, SO I DIDN'T HAVE MUCH OF A CHANCE TO THINK ABOUT IT.
BUT WHEN I WAS IN FOURTH GRADE, MY TEACHER WAS VERY KIND, GENEROUS, AND TOLERANT...
HE WAS, IN A WAY, HOW AN IDEAL FATHER WOULD BE...
THAT WAS PROBABLY THE FIRST TIME I GOT A REALLY STRONG SENSE OF WHAT A FATHER WAS...
I WOULD THINK... "IF I COULD HAVE A FATHER, HE WOULD BE A REALLY GOOD ONE..."
I WANTED TO BECOME MY TEACHER'S FAVORITE STUDENT... AND, WELL, I WAS ALREADY PRETTY BRIGHT.
SO I WORKED HARD AND BECAME AN HONOR STUDENT.
MY TEACHER GREW TO LIKE ME EVEN MORE THAN THE REST OF THE STUDENTS...

THEN ONE DAY, MY TEACHER HAD ME STAY AFTER SCHOOL.
WHEN HE CAME IN, HE WASN'T HOW HE USUALLY WAS. SOMETHING WAS DIFFERENT...
HE SEEMED NERVOUS, AND HE WAS BREATHING HEAVILY.
AND WITH A SWEATY HAND, HE GRABBED MY SHOULDER FIRMLY...
AND THEN HE...
WHAT THEN?!
OH MY GOD! JUST LIKE I THOUGHT!

HE BOWED HIS HEAD AND BEGGED ME TO LET HIM MARRY MY MOTHER.

HUH?
WHAT?
YOUR MOTHER?

IT WOULD APPEAR HE'D BEEN HARBORING A LOVE FOR HER WITHOUT ME EVEN KNOWING ABOUT IT.

SINCE I'D ALWAYS THOUGHT OF HIM AS AN IDEAL FATHER ANYWAY, I SAID "OKAY."

SOON AS HE WASN'T MY TEACHER ANYMORE, AND AFTER A LOT OF DISCUSSION, THEY GOT MARRIED.

THEN THEY HAD MY LITTLE BROTHER. NOW IT'S A HAPPY FAMILY FULL OF DREAMS AND ALL THAT JUNK.

...WAIT A SECOND...

WHAT ABOUT THE LOVE-HATE DRAMA? DON'T YOU HAVE A DARK PAST?

NOPE.

YOU MADE SUCH A BIG DEAL OF TELLING ME, AND THAT'S ALL THIS IS ABOUT?!

UGH, C'MON.

DON'T GET SO ANGRY. THAT'S WHY I TOLD YOU BEFOREHAND NOT TO ACT DIFFERENTLY NO MATTER WHAT I TOLD YOU.

THAT SOUNDS LIKE YOU WANT ME TO ACCEPT YOU DESPITE SOME SORT OF HORRIBLE PAST!!

GOD...

SIGH

はぁー…

SO WHY DON'T YOU WANT TO GO HOME IF IT'S SUCH A "HAPPY FAMILY FULL OF DREAMS"?

...BECAUSE THAT DOESN'T INCLUDE ME...

WHAT...?
IT'S NOT... THAT I'M AGAINST GOING HOME...
IT'S JUST... I DON'T WANT TO LOOK AT MY FAMILY AND FEEL LIKE I'M AN OUTSIDER.
AN OUTSIDER ...?
IT WAS FINE WHEN I WAS WITH MY MOTHER. WE'RE RELATED BY BLOOD, SO I FELT THAT FAMILY BOND.
IT WAS ALL RIGHT WHEN MY TEACHER BECAME MY STEP-FATHER. MY MOTHER AND I WEREN'T RELATED TO HIM, BUT IT WAS THE SIMPLEST WAY TO FORM A FAMILY.
THEN THEY HAD MY BROTHER AND THINGS DIDN'T WORK THAT WAY ANYMORE.
THAT'S THE NORMAL WAY TO FORM A FAMILY... TWO UNRELATED PEOPLE GET MARRIED AND HAVE A CHILD.

NOW WHEN I SEE THE THREE OF THEM TOGETHER, I THINK...
"AHH... THEY'RE A PERFECT FAMILY..."
IF I WERE THERE TOO, IT WOULDN'T FEEL NATURAL. IF ANYTHING, MY BEING THERE WOULD MAKE IT *IMPERFECT*.
WHEN I REALIZED THAT, I FELT LIKE I WAS NOTHING MORE THAN DEAD WEIGHT TO MY FAMILY.

BUT WHY? YOU'RE STILL RELATED TO YOUR MOTHER, AND YOUR BROTHER HAS THE SAME BLOOD.
YOU HAVE EVERY RIGHT TO BE A PART OF THAT FAMILY. WHY CAN'T YOU OPENLY BE WITH THEM?
OR WAS IT...
...THAT THEY WERE COLD TO YOU?

...NO... NOTHING LIKE THAT.
BUT...
FOR A NEWLY MARRIED COUPLE, THERE'S A SPACE YOU CAN'T PENETRATE NO MATTER WHO YOU ARE.
AND WHEN THEY HAVE A CHILD, THE CHILD BECOMES THAT FAMILY'S WORLD.
I UNDERSTOOD ALL OF THAT. BUT EVEN SO, I COULDN'T HELP BUT FEEL ALIENATED.

MAYBE I SHOULD HAVE TRIED TO GET CLOSER IF THAT'S HOW I FELT... BUT I JUST COULDN'T...

WHY ARE YOU SO SHY ABOUT IT?

YOU'RE RIGHT...
I WAS PROBABLY WRONG ABOUT IT FROM THE START...
...LIKE PUTTING A BUTTON IN THE WRONG HOLE ON A SHIRT...
I REALLY WAS HAPPY THAT THEY MARRIED EACH OTHER. THEY WERE THE PEOPLE I LOVED MOST.
BUT AT THE SAME TIME, THERE WAS AN HONEST SADNESS DEEP DOWN INSIDE ME.
I FELT LIKE MY TEACHER HAD STOLEN MY MOTHER... AND MY MOTHER HAD STOLEN MY TEACHER. I FELT LIKE I'D BEEN THROWN AWAY BY BOTH OF THEM.
IT BOTHERED ME THAT THEY DIDN'T TELL ME THEY'D BEEN SEEING EACH OTHER.
AND I THOUGHT THAT MAYBE THE REASON THEY HID IT WAS BECAUSE THEY FELT LIKE I WAS IN THE WAY...
I WANTED TO KNOW THE TRUTH, BUT I WAS ALSO AFRAID OF IT. SO I TRIED TO DENY THAT FEELING,
AND I TOOK ON AN ATTITUDE THAT ON THE SURFACE WAS FUN AND HAPPY...
I SEE IT NOW...

EVER SINCE THEN I'VE HAD A SORT OF LINGERING GRUDGE DEEP INSIDE OF ME... AND IT KEEPS ME FROM GETTING CLOSE TO THEM...
I KNOW NOW WHAT MAKES HIM SEEM SO MUCH LIKE ME...
AREN'T YOU THE ONE WHO CREATED THAT FEELING OF BEING ALIEN-ATED?
JUST LIKE ME...
YEAH... I GUESS YOU'RE RIGHT...
HE TOO LOST HIS "PLACE", AND THAT'S WHY HE CAME HERE.
EVEN SO, I'M SURPRISED. I NEVER THOUGHT YOU OF ALL PEOPLE WOULD BE THIS NEGATIVE...
AT SCHOOL YOU'VE GOT SUCH A BRAZEN ATTITUDE AND MANAGE PEOPLE SO EASILY.
YET WHEN IT COMES TO YOUR FAMILY YOU BECOME SO FRAGILE AND VULNERABLE ...
I'M NOT SURE WHY...
I DON'T HAVE TO CARE WHAT ANYONE AT SCHOOL WILL THINK ABOUT THE WAY I ACT...
BUT I'M DEATHLY AFRAID OF BEING ALIENATED FROM MY FAMILY... IT REALLY SCARES ME.
ANYTHING BUT MY FAMILY...

OH, OKAY. YEAH... I SEE NOW.

BECAUSE ULTIMATELY, YOUR FAMILY AND YOUR HOME ARE YOUR ONLY SHELTER...

YOU NEVER HAVE TO THINK ABOUT WHETHER OR NOT YOU'RE PROTECTED... I MEAN UNLESS SOMETHING BAD HAPPENS.

I DIDN'T THINK ABOUT IT EITHER UNTIL I LOST MY PARENTS.

UNTIL SAYAKA GOT TO BE HOW SHE IS, I'D ALWAYS THOUGHT OF MY UNCLE'S HOUSE AS MY SHELTER...

EVEN THOUGH SOMETIMES IT WASN'T QUITE THE SAME...

THAT'S WHY IT MAKES SENSE FOR YOU TO FEAR LOSING IT.

WHY DON'T YOU TELL THEM? TELL YOUR FAMILY EVERYTHING THAT MAKES YOU SCARED.
WOULDN'T NOW BE THE BEST TIME? IF YOU TALK ABOUT IT LIKE IT'S SOMETHING FROM A LONG TIME AGO, IT WON'T HURT LIKE IT DID THEN. YOU WERE ABLE TO TELL *ME,* WEREN'T YOU?
WHAT, NOW? BUT THIS WAS ALL SIX YEARS AGO...
WITH ALL THINGS, IF YOU LET A CHANCE PASS YOU BY, AND DON'T DO ANYTHING ABOUT IT, IT'S EASY TO THINK IT'S TOO LATE.
BUT THERE'S NO LIMIT TO WHEN YOU CAN FIX THINGS.

SO EVEN IF YOU THINK IT'S TOO LATE, IF YOU PUT A BUTTON THROUGH THE WRONG HOLE ON YOUR SHIRT, YOU CAN STILL TAKE OFF YOUR SHIRT.
THEN YOU CAN JUST PUT IT ON AGAIN AND GET IT RIGHT.
...AND IF FOR SOME REASON THINGS DON'T WORK OUT, THERE'S ALWAYS THIS PLACE.
YOU CAN ALWAYS COME BACK HERE.
I MAY NOT BE ABLE TO HEAL YOUR WOUNDS...
BUT I WILL ALWAYS LISTEN JUST LIKE I AM NOW. AND IF YOU WANT ME BY YOUR SIDE, THEN I'LL BE THERE.
TOHRU...

OR AM I NOT GOOD ENOUGH?

HE HE

HMMM...

JUST ONE THING, TOHRU... YOU SOUND LIKE YOU'RE TALKING TO YOUR LOVER, OR SOMETHING.

WHA...

I WAS JUST TRYING TO MAKE YOU FEEL BETTER...!

WAS THAT FROM A SOAP OPERA?

I'M FLATTERED THAT YOU WOULD HIT ON ME, BUT LET'S KEEP OUR RELATIONSHIP PLATONIC.

'KAY?

I'M NOT TRYING TO HOOK UP WITH YOU!!

AND I'M THE ONE THAT WANTS IT PLATONIC. YOU'RE THE ONE WHO KISSED ME!!

AND SO, BEFORE VACATION ENDED, YUUJIROU REMOVED HIS SHIRT WITH THE BUTTON IN THE WRONG HOLE, AND RETURNED HOME TO HIS FAMILY.

WHEN HE COMES BACK NEXT SEMESTER, I SHOULD BE ABLE TO TELL BY HIS EXPRESSION WHETHER OR NOT HE WAS ABLE TO SET THINGS RIGHT.

TO BE CONTINUED IN PRINCESS • PRINCESS VOLUME 3

THIS NEXT PART IS THE PRINCESS • PRINCESS SIDE STORY. IT'S ABOUT KOUNO AND SHIHOUDANI GOING TO SAKAMOTO'S HOUSE DURING VACATION.
MIKOTO STILL ISN'T BACK YET, THOUGH.
HE'S WITH HIS GIRLFRIEND! (HA HA)

TAKA-TAK
TAKA-TOK
WE MADE IT TO THE STATION, BUT WHERE'S THE EXIT?
FWIP
KOUNO AND SHIHOUDANI ARE ON VACATION.
OH, IT'S OVER HERE. HE SAID TO TAKE THE NORTH GATE.
THEY CHOSE TO STAY AT THE DORMITORY INSTEAD OF GOING HOME, SO THEY HAVE PLENTY OF FREE TIME.
KA-CHT
AND TODAY THEY DECIDED TO SPEND THE NIGHT AT SAKAMOTO'S HOUSE.
OH!
OVER HERE, GUYS.
Princess·Princess SIDE STORY

プリンセス・プリンセス
PRINCESS · PRINCESS

SIDE STORY

THANKS FOR COMING OUT TO PICK US UP.
OH, NO PROBLEM. IT'S ONLY ABOUT A TEN-MINUTE WALK.

SO, IS THE ORIGINAL "SAKAMOTO-SAMA" WE'VE HEARD SO MUCH ABOUT GOING TO BE THERE?

YEAH! WE WANT TO SEE HIM!

LEAN

ER... I'M NOT SURE...
I DON'T THINK HE WAS HOME WHEN I LEFT...

AND, UMM...
TRY NOT TO BE TOO SURPRISED WHEN WE GET THERE...
?

THIS IS MY HOUSE.

BA-BAAAAHM

HAA...
IT'S HUGE...
IT'S A TWO-STORY HOUSE. AND A REALLY NICE ONE, TOO.

SAKA-MOTO... ARE YOU...
FILTHY RICH?
UGH
NO, NOTHING LIKE THAT. MY FATHER HAS A JOB DOING ARCHITECTURE. THAT'S WHY IT'S ONLY OUR HOUSE THAT'S NICE.
BUT ANYWAY, COME ON UP.
LET'S GET INSIDE AND HAVE A COOL DRINK. YOU MUST BE HOT.
YEAH, THAT SOUNDS *GREAT*.
I'M SO THIRSTY!
GA-CHAK
SHOULD WE TAKE OUR SHOES OFF?
I'M HOME!
AKI-CHAN, ARE YOUR FRIENDS HERE?
FLAP

YEAH, THIS IS KOUNO AND SHIHOUDANI.

HELLO! MAKE YOURSELVES AT HOME.

HELLO...

NICE TO MEET YOU...

WAH... FOR SOME REASON... I SEE FLOWERS...

WE'RE USUALLY THE ONES WITH FLOWERS...

I'LL BRING YOU SOME COLD DRINKS. SHOULD I TAKE THEM TO YOUR ROOM?

YES, PLEASE.

MY ROOM'S ON THE SECOND FLOOR, SO LET'S HEAD UP.

YEAH...

OKAY...

WAS THAT YOUR OLDER SISTER? SHE'S PRETTY CUTE.
COULD BE A MODEL SOMEDAY...
DON'T YOU MEAN *LITTLE* SISTER? SHE WAS TINY!
!!
FLINCH

NO, SHE GREETED US SO POLITELY! SHE HAS TO BE HIS OLDER SISTER.
SHE WAS LIKE A LITTLE BABY CHICK! TOTALLY HIS LITTLE SISTER.
WHY DON'T WE JUST ASK HIM?
FINE! HEY, SAKAMOTO!

WHICH IS THE RIGHT ANSWER?!

UMM...
THAT PERSON IS...

I'M HIS *MOTHER.*

...YEAH.

HIS MOTHER?!

NO WAY!

I HOPE YOU DON'T MIND MY ASKING... IS SHE AN IN-LAW?
SHE'S MY REAL MOM.
DEAD SERIOUS
WHAT? WOW! HOW OLD IS SHE?!
SHE LOOKS REALLY YOUNG, BUT SHE'S 43. EVEN THEN...
THAT'S WITHOUT PLASTIC SURGERY OR ANYTHING...
WOOOW...

I'M SO SURPRISED! I NEVER THOUGHT HIS MOM WOULD BE LIKE THAT...
I THOUGHT SHE'D BE QUIETER.
LIKE A TRADITIONAL JAPANESE MOM.
THERE'S STILL PLENTY OF SURPRIS-ES...
MUTTER

HM? DID YOU SAY SOME-THING?
OH, UHH... NO!
KNOCK
KNOCK
AH, COME IN!
GA-CHAK

AKI-CHAN, DO YOU HAVE A SEC?
PEEK
!!
OH...
SORRY.
I DIDN'T KNOW YOU HAD PEOPLE OVER.
I'LL ASK YOU ABOUT IT LATER.
PULL
AH!
NO! PLEASE DON'T PAY US ANY MIND!
PLEASE, CARRY ON WITH WHATEVER YOU WERE GOING TO DO.
WAIT, WAIT?
PLEASE.
OH... YOU SURE?
ALL RIGHT...

WHISPER ボソッ
HE'S REALLY GOOD LOOKING...
WHISPER ボソッ
YEAH, DEFINITELY HIS LITTLE BROTHER. HE CERTAINLY LOOKS YOUNGER THAN SAKAMOTO-SAMA.
WHISPER ボソッ
BUT HIS MOM REALLY THREW US OFF, SO WE MIGHT NOT BE ABLE TO TELL FROM THE OUTSIDE.
WHISPER ボソッ
YOU THINK THAT'S HIS OLDER BROTHER? OR HIS DAD? PROBABLY NOT, SINCE HE'S ASKING FOR HELP ON HIS HOMEWORK.
WHISPER ボソッ
HMM... I DON'T KNOW...
WHISPER ボソッ
MAYBE IT'S NOT FOR SCHOOL...
CAN YOU SHOW ME HOW TO DO THIS ONE?
THANKS, AKI-CHAN.
SORRY FOR INTRUDING.
ペコッ NOD
NO, NO...
WE'RE THE ONES WHO ARE INTRUDING.
BATAM パタン…

WELL? WAS THAT YOUR LITTLE BROTHER?
WAS IT?
NO, UHH... THAT WAS...
WAH
LEAN
OR WAS IT YOUR OLDER BROTHER? OR YOUR DAD?
THAT WAS MY LITTLE SISTER...
YOUR SISTER ?!
NO WAY! SHE DIDN'T SEEM LIKE A GIRL AT ALL! EVEN THE WAY SHE TALKED...
EVEN IF SHE WAS ATTRAC-TIVE...
SHE DIDN'T GIVE OFF THAT SOFT VIBE THAT GIRLS USUALLY DO. AND AFTER SEEING YOUR MOM, SHE DOESN'T SEEM LIKE A GIRL IN COMPARISON...
SHE'S LIKE THAT NOW, BUT A FEW YEARS AGO SHE HAD LONG HAIR, AND THE WAY SHE TALKED... WAS STILL A LITTLE FEMININE.
SOMETHING HAPPENED AND SHE CHANGED ALL OF A SUDDEN...
SHE USED TO LOOK LIKE THIS.

SHUDDER
IT DOESN'T GET ANY STRANGER FROM HERE ON, THOUGH, RIGHT?
HA HA HA HA

HIS MOM WAS LIKE THAT... AND HIS SISTER'S LIKE *THAT*...
AND THEN THERE'S HIS OLDER BROTHER, WHO CONTROLLED THE WHOLE SCHOOL...
YOU'VE GOT A LOT OF ABNORMAL PEOPLE IN YOUR FAMILY...
I GUESS YOU COULD SAY BIZARRE...

WAIT... DON'T TELL ME IT GETS... EVEN STRANGER...
IS YOUR DAD...?
N...
NO!

MY *DAD'S* NORMAL!
...
...
...I THINK... MAYBE...
NO... WELL...
SORT OF...

SAKAMOTO, YOU CAN'T REALLY SAY YOUR DAD'S NORMAL IF YOU HAVE TO SAY "I THINK" AND "MAYBE" TOO.
SOMETHING TELLS ME THERE ARE MORE PEOPLE LEFT THAN JUST YOUR DAD... WHO ELSE DO YOU HAVE IN YOUR FAMILY? ARE *THEY* NORMAL?
GAAAAAAAH!
OHHH...
KNOCK
KNOCK
AGAIN?!
JUMP
UM, COME IN.
WHO WILL IT BE THIS TIME...?

I'VE GOT IT! THE VIBE I'M GETTING FROM HIS STRANGE AURA MEANS IT HAS TO BE THE LEGENDARY SAKAMOTO-SAMA! THEREFORE, YOU MUST HIS OLDER BROTHER!

FFT

PSHT

IT'S BEEN SOMETHING UNEXPECTED EVERY TIME SO FAR... I THINK THE ANSWER IS SOMETHING COUNTER-INTUITIVE LIKE HIS GRANDMOTHER! IN FACT, I BET YOU'RE HIS GRANDMOTHER ON HIS MOTHER'S SIDE AND YOU LOOK SO YOUNG BECAUSE IT RUNS IN YOUR FAMILY! WELL??

SORRY BOYS, YOU'RE BOTH WRONG. I'M HIS ***OLDER SISTER***.

YOU'RE PRETTY CUTE, BUT YOU'RE BOTH SO STRANGE.
HA HA HA HA
OLDER SISTER...?
SHE OBVIOUSLY DOESN'T REALIZE HOW WEIRD SHE IS...
HAVING HER CALL US WEIRD ISN'T RIGHT...

WELL, THAT WORKS OUT PERFECT, THEN. YOU AND YOUR FRIENDS CAN EAT THESE.
THEY'RE PROBABLY COOKIES...
FFFWOOP
AH!

SAKAMOTO, YOU CAN'T REALLY SAY YOUR DAD'S NORMAL IF YOU HAVE TO SAY "I THINK" AND "MAYBE" TOO.

SOMETHING TELLS ME THERE ARE MORE PEOPLE LEFT THAN JUST YOUR DAD... WHO ELSE DO YOU HAVE IN YOUR FAMILY? ARE *THEY* NORMAL?

GAAAAAAAH!

OHHH...

KNOCK

KNOCK

AGAIN?!

JUMP

GA-CHAK
HEY AKIRA. SOMEONE BROUGHT ME SWEETS, BUT I'M NOT HUNGRY.
OH, WE HAVE GUESTS.
FRIENDS OF YOURS?
ANOTHER GORGEOUS FAMILY MEMBER... WHO IS IT??
IS IT A GUY? A GIRL? IT'S HARD TO TELL WITH THIS ONE, TOO!!

UMM...
THIS IS MY UHH...
STOP!
WAIT WAIT WAIT! DON'T SAY ANY-THING!
DON'T TELL US! WE'LL TRY TO GUESS.
O... OKAY...
UHHH... IT'S UHH...
THAT'S UMM...
HE DIDN'T CALL HIM "AKI-CHAN" SO HE'S PROBABLY OLDER...
AND WE COULDN'T TELL AGE OR GENDER FOR SAKAMOTO'S MOM AND SISTER, SO WE CAN'T RELY ON LOOKS.
BUT THAT MEANS IT'S HIS DAD, HIS OLDER BROTHER, OR HIS OLDER SISTER. THERE'S ALSO THE CHANCE THAT IT COULD BE SOMEONE RIDICULOUS, LIKE ONE OF HIS GRANDPARENTS...

I'VE GOT IT! THE VIBE I'M GETTING FROM HIS STRANGE AURA MEANS IT HAS TO BE THE LEGENDARY SAKAMOTO-SAMA! THEREFORE, YOU MUST HIS OLDER BROTHER!

FFT

PSHT

IT'S BEEN SOMETHING UNEXPECTED EVERY TIME SO FAR... I THINK THE ANSWER IS SOMETHING COUNTER-INTUITIVE LIKE HIS GRANDMOTHER! IN FACT, I BET YOU'RE HIS GRANDMOTHER ON HIS MOTHER'S SIDE AND YOU LOOK SO YOUNG BECAUSE IT RUNS IN YOUR FAMILY! WELL??

SORRY BOYS, YOU'RE BOTH WRONG. I'M HIS OLDER SISTER.

YOU'RE PRETTY CUTE, BUT YOU'RE BOTH SO STRANGE.
HA HA HA HA
OLDER SISTER...?
SHE OBVIOUSLY DOESN'T REALIZE HOW WEIRD SHE IS...
HAVING HER CALL US WEIRD ISN'T RIGHT...

WELL, THAT WORKS OUT PERFECT, THEN. YOU AND YOUR FRIENDS CAN EAT THESE.
THEY'RE PROBABLY COOKIES...
FFFWOOP
AH!

YOU GUYS HAVE FUN!
WAVE
ひら
WAVE
ひら

PATAM
パタンッ…

SAKA-MOTO...
ビクッ
FLINCH
Y-YEAH?

HOW MANY PEOPLE *ARE* THERE IN YOUR FAMILY?
JUST GIVE US A NUMBER. DON'T START DRAWING YOUR FAMILY TREE.
UM...

THERE'S... SIX PEOPLE IN MY FAMILY...
AND ONE CAT...

OKAY! THAT LEAVES YOUR DAD AND YOUR OLDER BROTHER!

SO THE NEXT PERSON WILL BE A DUEL.

HEH HEH HEH

TING

WAIT, WHY IS THIS TURNING INTO A DUEL?!

AND SINCE WHEN?

HELLO!
!!
MORE TWINKLING!
HELLO...
IS THIS HIS BROTHER? OR HIS DAD? HE LOOKS TOO YOUNG TO BE HIS DAD!
IF THIS IS HIS DAD, THEN WE'RE LOOKING AT A NEVER-AGING COUPLE HERE. THEY MAY BE ABNORMAL, BUT THAT'S JUST NOT POSSIBLE.
SO DOES THAT MEAN IT'S HIS BROTHER?
AH, I'M AKIRA'S ...
FWUMP
QUIET! WE'RE THINKING!
HE DOESN'T REALLY HAVE THAT NOBLE AIR ABOUT HIM THAT SOMEONE WHO CONTROLLED THE SCHOOL MIGHT HAVE... BUT HE'S CERTAINLY HANDSOME.
HUH ...?
WHAT IN THE
WORLD?
SORRY
THEN AGAIN, HE LOOKS PRETTY CHARMING, AND BEING SO EASY TO GET ALONG WITH, HE COULD PROBABLY GET PEOPLE TO FOLLOW HIM...

WAIT, WHAT THE HELL? EVERY SINGLE PERSON IN HIS FAMILY IS INSANELY GOOD-LOOKING. ARE THEY USING SOME SORT OF SPECIAL TECHNIQUE?

BAM
ANYWAY!
OKAY, SO WE'VE REACHED OUR VERDICT. YOU ARE THE LEGENDARY SAKAMOTO-SAMA, AND THEREFORE YOU'RE HIS BROTHER!
WELL?
WHATEVER.
SO, ANYWAY.

NOOO! I'M SORRY, I'M NOT HIM.
HA HA HA HA
>HE HE< THEY THINK I'M YOUR BROTHER! ♪
THIS IS MY DAD...
YOUR DAD?!

HMPH

SO THAT MEANS YOU'RE MARRIED TO HIS MOM?! NEITHER OF YOU LOOK A DAY OVER 20!!
HOW OLD ARE YOU?
THERE'S A LIMIT TO HOW ALIKE TWO PEOPLE CAN BE. IF YOU REALLY ARE PARENTS THEN THESE COULDN'T POSSIBLY BE YOUR KIDS.
YOU EVEN REACT JUST LIKE HER.
I ASSURE YOU THEY'RE OUR CHILDREN. I GET THAT QUITE OFTEN, ACTUALLY... PEOPLE SAYING OUR FAMILY IS A LITTLE STRANGE...
I THINK WE'RE NORMAL.
HMM...
"A LITTLE"? YEAH RIGHT. YOU'RE ALL CRAZY.
I WONDER WHY...
NORMAL MY ASS.
WELL, ANYWAY, YOU HAVE FUN TOGETHER.
BYE NOW.
PATAM
...

BUT ***YOUR ENTIRE FAMILY*** HAS GOT ME ***REALLY PUMPED UP!***

SO MUCH THAT MY HEART IS RACING!

>HA HA HA< ...

YEAH, ME TOO.

MY PALMS ARE ALL SWEATY.

BUT YOU'VE LIVED WITH THIS FAMILY YOUR WHOLE LIFE, RIGHT?

YOU NEVER THOUGHT YOUR FAMILY WAS WEIRD...? OR STRANGE...? OR EVEN JUST NOT ***NORMAL?*** NOT EVEN ONCE?

WELL... I GUESS IF IT'S YOUR OWN FAMILY IT WOULDN'T REALLY COME TO MIND...

NO, THAT'S NOT TRUE...
BUT...
ふるっ
SHAKE
IT'S NOT THAT I THOUGHT THEY WEREN'T NORMAL... I JUST THOUGHT ABOUT HOW I'M SO DIFFERENT FROM THEM.

I MEAN, LOOK HOW PLAIN MY FACE IS. DO I LOOK LIKE I'M RELATED TO THE REST OF MY FAMILY?
I LOOK LIKE I WAS ADOPTED.
AH...
NO, YOU-- I MEAN, YOU DO...

YOU DON'T HAVE TO BE POLITE. YOU CAN TELL JUST BY LOOKING. I'VE HEARD IT SINCE I WAS A KID.
EVERYONE AROUND HERE SAYS SO.
WOW...

THERE WAS A TIME WHERE I WAS REALLY STRESSED OUT AND UPSET ABOUT IT...

SOMETIMES I FELT LIKE I WAS AN OUTSIDER...

AND IT MADE ME THINK, "IS IT OKAY FOR ME TO BE HERE?"... "WOULD THEY BE BETTER OFF IF I WASN'T AROUND?"

THAT'S WHEN I REALIZED...
EVEN THOUGH MY FAMILY DID LOVE ME, ALL I WOULD LISTEN TO WAS WHAT PEOPLE SAID... I WASN'T LOOKING AT WHAT WAS REALLY IMPORTANT.
I WAS THE ONE WHO CONCEIVED THAT MY FAMILY DIDN'T WANT ME...

THAT'S WHY I HAVE TO HOLD MY HEAD HIGH AND BELIEVE.
AS LONG AS I DO, WHAT'S MOST IMPORTANT TO ME AND WHERE I BELONG WILL ALWAYS BE CLEAR...
WHEN I REALIZED THAT, I FELT SO MUCH BETTER.

IN THE END...
IT WAS ALL UP TO ME...

I SEE NOW.
OH, I SEE NOW!
THE REASON SAKAMOTO-SAMA LOOKS LIKE HE'S OVERCOME A LIFE OF HARDSHIP AND EARNED ETERNAL PEACE IS BECAUSE HE'S ACHIEVED ENLIGHTENMENT.
I HAVEN'T ACHIEVED *ENLIGHTENMENT*.
GUYS, I'M NOTHING SPECIAL.
ALL I DID WAS NOTICE IT WAS BETTER TO FLIP OUT ABOUT IT THAN TO KEEP HOLDING IT ALL INSIDE.
NO GOOD HOLDING IT IN.
FLIP OUT...?
ISN'T THAT A LITTLE EXTREME?
WHAT I MEAN IS... HMM, HERE'S A GOOD EXAMPLE.
SHIHOUDANI, IF YOU DON'T MIND, I'D LIKE YOU TO STOP SAYING "SAMA" AFTER MY NAME.
ER...
HAS THAT BEEN BOTHERING YOU?
OH, YEAH. HASN'T HE ASKED THAT BEFORE?
BUT I DON'T SAY IT TO BE DISTANT OR UNFRIENDLY TOWARD YOU.
I KNOW YOU DON'T.
BUT WHEN YOU PUT "SAMA" ON MY NAME, IT FEELS LIKE THERE'S AN INVISIBLE WALL BETWEEN US.
I FEEL LIKE WE'RE TALKING ON OPPOSITE SIDES OF A GLASS WALL.
I CAN'T GET *EVERYONE* TO STOP DOING IT, SO I'VE GIVEN UP ON TRYING...
BUT I AT LEAST DON'T WANT TO FEEL THAT WAY WITH THE PEOPLE I'M CLOSE TO.

RIGHT, THEN. I'LL CALL YOU SAKAMOTO, JUST AS TOHRU DOES.
HANG ON!
IF WE'RE GONNA USE HIS NAME, WHY NOT USE HIS FIRST NAME LIKE WE DO WITH EACH OTHER?
THIS IS CRUCIAL!

OR WOULD YOU RATHER WE USED "SAKA-MOTO"?
NO, THAT'S JUST FINE!
ALL RIGHT! THEN FROM NOW ON, INSTEAD OF SAKAMOTO-SAMA, WE'LL CALL YOU AKIRA.
YOU GO AHEAD AND USE OUR FIRST NAMES, TOO.
S-SURE!

LET'S TRY IT OUT.
CALL ME TOHRU.
AND CALL ME YUU-JIROU.
GO ON. SAY IT.

UMM...
TOHRU...
YUUJI-ROU...

カーッ...
BLUSHHH

I FEEL... A LITTLE EMBAR-RASSED...
ひゃー
WHOO
FOR SOME REASON...
IT'S ALWAYS A LITTLE STRANGE AT FIRST.
YEAH, YOU'LL GET USED TO IT.
IT FEELS KINDA WEIRD HEARING IT...
OKAY, NOW IT'S OUR TURN.
AKI...
1, 2, 3...
AKIRAAA!!!!
バーンッ
BAM

LISTEN, TODAY WE WENT OUT WITH SOME GIRLS, AND THE GUYS STAYED RIGHT NEXT TO ME THE WHOLE TIME! I COULDN'T GET ***NEAR*** THE GIRLS!

I'M POSITIVE THEY WERE DOING IT ON PURPOSE! DON'T YOU THINK THAT'S MEAN?

C-CALM DOWN, ***HARU***.

OKAY?

IT'S... IT'S HIS BROTHER...

THIS GUY IS THE LEGENDARY SAKAMOTO-SAMA...

I'VE, UMM... I'VE GOT SOME FRIENDS OVER RIGHT NOW...
SEE...?
AH...

WAAAH!
HI, THERE...
HELLO.

HE WAS DEFINITELY HANDSOME...

IF HE WAS A GIRL, HE COULD LIVE OFF JUST BEING BEAUTIFUL.

SERIOUSLY.

BUT HE ACTUALLY LOOKS HIS AGE...
LIKE AN OLDER BROTHER WOULD...
AND IT'S NOT DIFFICULT TO TELL HE'S A GUY...
IT'S FAIRLY OBVIOUS.

FLUSTERED

SEEING HIM COME IN LIKE THAT...
DOESN'T REALLY SEEM LIKE THE CHARISMATIC, MYSTERIOUS TYPE THAT WOULD BECOME A LEGEND...

AFTER SEEING HIS ENTIRE FAMILY FULL OF STRANGE PEOPLE, SEEING A GUY THAT'S JUST HANDSOME SEEMS COMPLETELY NORMAL...

WHOA, HANG ON.

I WOULD NORMALLY BE SURPRISED...

GAH, WE'RE DESENSITIZED...

STILL...
BEING IN A FAMILY WHERE EVERYONE IS BEAUTIFUL KINDA MAKES YOU ABNORMAL, TOO.
YEAH, YOU'RE ABNORMAL BY EXTENSION.
OHOOO

JUST THEN, AKIRA THOUGHT, "HEY, AREN'T THEY FOR-GETTING THAT THEY'RE REALLY ATTRACTIVE, TOO?"
......

AND ON THAT DAY DURING VACATION...
THEY BECAME MUCH CLOSER TO SAKAMOTO THAN BEFORE.
AND THEY RETURNED TO THEIR DORMITORY HAVING DISCOVERED THAT SAKAMOTO'S WHOLE FAMILY IS WEIRD.

ADDITIONALLY...
ON THAT SAME DAY, MIKOTO WENT OUT ON A DATE WITH HIS GIRLFRIEND ...
BUT, AS ALWAYS, HE WAS UNABLE TO FIND ANY PRIVACY.
YOU KNOW HOW IT IS.
KA-BOOM
どかーんっ
MARCH MARCH
ぞろぞろ
HE HE HE
HA HA HA
I THOUGHT I TOLD YOU NOT TO FOLLOW ME!

PRINCESS • PRINCESS SIDE STORY ✹ END

HELLO! I'D FIRST LIKE TO SAY... IT'S NOT MIKIO TSUDA, IT'S NOT KIYOMI TSUDA, AND IT'S NOT EVEN KIYO TSUDAMI... IT'S *MIKIYO TSUDA*.
SO MANY PEOPLE GOT IT WRONG...
"TAISHI ZAOU" IS RIGHT, THOUGH. THAT'S ME, TOO.
AFTERWORD

HONESTLY, I WAS WORRIED HOW THIS STORY WOULD BE RECEIVED, SINCE THERE'S NO FEMALE MAIN CHARACTER, EVEN THOUGH IT *IS* A SHOUJO MANGA.
FORGET GIRLS, WILL THEY LIKE THE GUYS?
I MEAN, I'VE GOT A LOT OF MALE READERS...
うーん...
HMM
TURNS OUT I HAD NO NEED TO WORRY.
ALL OF YOU WENT WILD ABOUT SEEING MY OTHER CHARACTERS IN THE STORY.
Oh my god!! I'm so happy th
you put Mikoto in
Please put Kei and the other four in too!!
Anyway, thanks for using Mikoto!
Mikiyo-sama I was so surprised
o see Akira and
Koto!! But I
very happy to
them. Please
them doing
in the story!
IN FACT, THERE WERE PEOPLE THAT WERE DRAWN BY THE GOTHIC LOLITA DESIGNS ON THE COVER,
AND THOSE PEOPLE WANTED TO GET MY OTHER WORKS...
AND THEN!
ブラボー
MAGNIFICENT!!
ALL OF MY PREVIOUS WORKS WERE REPRINTED!!
EVEN TAISHI ZAOU STUFF!

I DIDN'T DO IT WITH THAT IN MIND AT ALL, BUT I'M GLAD I DID.
I CAN'T PLAN THAT FAR AHEAD.
THOUGH I *WAS* THINKING OF FANS OF *DAY OF REVOLUTION* AND *FAMILY COMPLEX* WHEN I MADE *PRINCESS • PRINCESS*.
I COMPLETELY FORGOT THAT NEW READERS WOULD COME FROM THERE.
I ONLY REALIZED IT WHEN THE REPRINT HAPPENED.
OH YEAH! THERE'S A WHOLE NEW GENERATION OF READERS!
WITHOUT EVEN THINKING ABOUT IT, I WENT BACK TO MAKE SURE I DREW THEM RIGHT.
FLIP FLIP FLIP
UMM UMM
SO I GUESS I SHOULD MENTION IT HERE.
A LITTLE LATE, BUT HERE'S AN AD.
MIKOTO IS THE MAIN SUPPORTING CHARACTER FROM DAY OF REVOLUTION, AND AKIRA IS THE MAIN CHARACTER FROM FAMILY COMPLEX. BOTH OF THEM ARE RELEASED BY WINGS COMICS, SO CHECK THEM OUT.*
ファミリー・コンプレックス

*ENGLISH VERSION OF *THE DAY OF REVOLUTION* IS AVAILABLE NOW FROM DIGITAL MANGA.

MOVING ON, I THOUGHT IT'D BE NICE IF I GOT SOME LETTERS WITH READERS' THOUGHTS, SO ON THE FIRST PRINTING I PUT IN A LITTLE NOTE OFFERING SOME DOUJINSHI. THE RESPONSE WAS TREMENDOUS.
TSUDA-SAN, IT'S AMAZING! LETTERS HAVE BEEN COMING TO THE OFFICE EVERY DAY! THEY DON'T STOP COMING!
CALL FROM THE RECEPTIONIST
WHOA! UH OH.. I HOPE THERE'S ENOUGH...
EIGHT OR NINE OUT OF TEN LETTERS HAD RETURN ENVELOPES IN THEM. I HAD NO IDEA THAT MANY PEOPLE WOULD WANT COPIES, SO I WENT PALE THINKING WE WOULDN'T HAVE ENOUGH.
SO WE PRINTED MORE...

WELL... IT WAS ROUGH, BUT IT WAS GREAT BEING ABLE TO READ EVERYONE'S OPINIONS.
PEOPLE WERE HAPPY ABOUT AKIRA AND MIKOTO.
A LOT OF PEOPLE WERE NERVOUS WRITING TO A MANGA ARTIST FOR THE FIRST TIME.
THE SALES RANKINGS WERE SURPRISING, TOO (CONSIDERING IT STILL GOT 4TH). THAT'S THE POWER OF MEDIA...

SO WHAT DO THE MAJORITY OF THE LETTERS SAY, YOU ASK?
EVERYONE LOVES ARISADA!
MIKOTO AND AKIRA, TOO, OF COURSE.
HUH?

I'M THE KIND OF PERSON WHO EASILY FORGETS WHAT THEY'VE JUST DRAWN.
NOT A GOOD THING FOR MANGA...
SO WHEN I HEARD THAT, I COULDN'T UNDERSTAND WHY A SUPPORTING CHARACTER LIKE ARISADA WOULD BE SO POPULAR...
AND BEFORE I KNEW IT I WAS LOOKING BACK THROUGH THE COMIC.

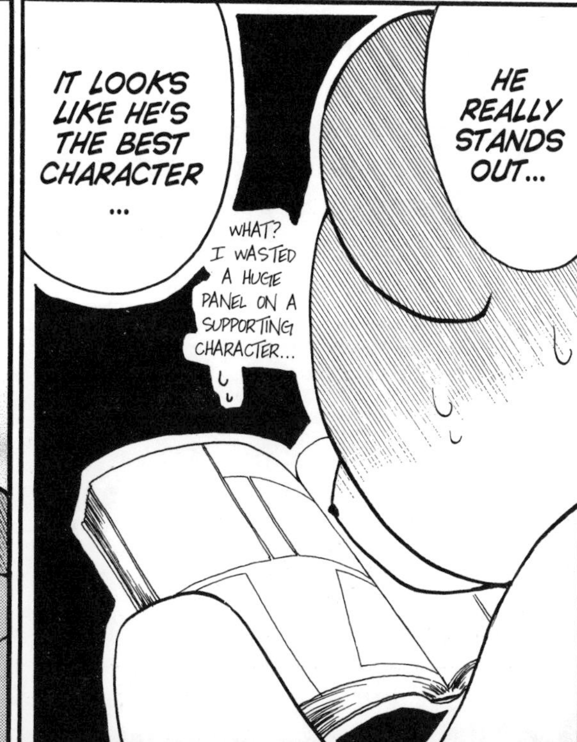
HE REALLY STANDS OUT...
IT LOOKS LIKE HE'S THE BEST CHARACTER ...
WHAT? I WASTED A HUGE PANEL ON A SUPPORTING CHARACTER...

I WAS KIND OF ASTOUNDED THAT I COULD NATURALLY DO SOMETHING SO AIR-HEADED.
I SERIOUSLY COULDN'T UNDERSTAND MYSELF.
WHAT WAS I THINKING WHEN I DREW THIS...?
I **DID** DRAW THIS, RIGHT?!
ずーん…
GLOOM

I THOUGHT I MIGHT SHARE SOME KNOWLEDGE ABOUT GOTHIC LOLITA FOR A MOMENT.
SOMETIMES PEOPLE CORRECT MY MISTAKES.
THE FRILLY OUTFITS THE PRINCESSES WORE AT THE DEBUT WERE LOLITA.
Lolita
"GOTH-LOLI" IS A TERM THAT COMES FROM "GOTHIC" AND "LOLITA", WHICH ARE TWO SEPARATE STYLES.
THE OUTFITS THEY WEAR ON THE COVERS ARE GOTHIC... SORT OF...
Gothic
BUT SOMETIMES THE TWO ARE MIXED, AND THERE ARE CERTAIN SUBTLETIES BETWEEN THEM.
MAYBE THEY CAME UP WITH "GOTH-LOLI" BECAUSE OF THE AMBIGUITY?!
THE MOST POPULAR GOTH-LOLI OUTFIT WAS THE NURSE ONE...
IT'S MORE LOLITA, BUT IF IT WERE BLACK, IT'D BE MORE GOTHIC.
POPULAR
No.1
OH, THAT'S RIGHT! SPEAKING OF THE NURSE OUTFIT, SOMETHING AMAZING HAPPENED!!
OKAY, GET THIS!

AT COMIC MARKET, THE BIGGEST EVENT IN WINTER, THERE WERE THREE GIRLS WEARING THE NURSE OUTFIT I'D DRAWN!!

HELLOOO! ♡

WOW, THAT'S INCREDIBLE! IT'S EXACTLY HOW I DREW IT!!

EVEN THE SANDALS AND MED-KIT!

AND AREN'T YOU COLD?! IT'S THE MIDDLE OF WINTER!!

OH!
OH!
LET ME TAKE A PICTURE !!
I HAVE MY CAMERA!
I DON'T LIKE HAVING MY PICTURE TAKEN, SO WHEN PEOPLE ASK I USUALLY REFUSE...
BUT THIS TIME I WAS SO EXCITED THAT I ASKED THEM MYSELF.
I HAPPENED TO HAVE MY CAMERA WITH ME, TOO.
PROOF

← I DIDN'T GET YOUR PERMISSION, SO PLEASE FORGIVE ME.

パシャッ
KACHINK

BUT THEN!
RIGHT AFTER THAT, ANOTHER GROUP WEARING THE NURSE OUTFIT CAME UP TO ME!
HELLOOO!
WAIT... WHAT?
YOU'RE NOT THE SAME GIRLS FROM BEFORE, ARE YOU?
THE TRIM IS A DIFFERENT COLOR...
THEY, TOO, WERE KIND ENOUGH TO LET ME TAKE A PICTURE.

ふうーーっ...
WHOOO
WOW... THAT WAS A SURPRISE. TWO GROUPS OF THREE?
WHY DOES EVERYONE COME IN GROUPS OF THREE?
THAT CONFUSED ME.

I MUST HAVE BEEN REALLY OUT OF IT. IT SERIOUSLY DIDN'T EVEN CROSS MY MIND HOW MANY PRINCESSES THERE WERE.
I WAS SO PRE-OCCUPIED WITH THE NURSE COSTUMES.
OOOH!
THAT'S WHY!
IT'S BECAUSE THERE ARE THREE PRINCESSES! THEY WERE DRESSED AS TOHRU, YUUJIROU, AND MIKOTO!
I THINK THEIR HAIR WAS DONE UP LIKE THEM, TOO!

IN VOLUME 2, THERE WEREN'T ANY NEW PRINCESS COSTUMES.
THEY WERE BUSY WITH OTHER THINGS.
I KNOW YOU WERE ALL EXPECTING NEW ONES. MY APOLOGIES. (HA HA)
I DIDN'T SHOW UP, EITHER.
IF I USE A DESIGN THAT DOESN'T HAVE VOLUME, THEN IT ISN'T AS FLOWERY, AND I CAN'T USE SOMETHING THAT SHOWS THE MALE BODYLINE.
SOMETIMES I IGNORE THAT RULE. (HA HA)
I WANT TO DRAW BOOBS.
BUT TRUTHFULLY, I'M A LITTLE SAD THAT THERE ARE LIMITS ON WHAT DESIGNS I CAN USE.
I WANT TO DRAW A TIGHT MINI-SKIRT.
THINGS NOT ALLOWED
PRETTY MUCH ANYTHING THAT DOESN'T WORK ON GUYS...
I WANT TO DRAW KNEE-HIGH SOCKS.
I GUESS THAT'S THE DOWN SIDE OF HAVING BOYS IN DRAG.
I'LL KEEP PUSHING THE LIMITS AND WILL HAVE A BRAND-NEW GOTH-LOLI COSTUME IN VOLUME 3.

HOW'D YOU KNOW ...?

HOW COULD I NOT KNOW?!

YOU ALWAYS DO THAT KIND OF THING.

I LIKE STORIES SET IN ALL-GIRLS SCHOOLS. IT'S LIKE A SPECIAL WORLD.

AND HAVING JUST GIRLS IS PRETTY.

EVEN MY OTHER STORIES LIKE FAMILY COMPLEX AND DAY OF REVOLUTION (ESSENTIALLY) HAVE ALL-GIRLS SCHOOLS.

THOUGH I DIDN'T GO TO AN ALL-GIRLS SCHOOL.

THOUGH THIS STORY IS ABOUT AN ALL-BOYS SCHOOL, I STILL GOT TO SPREAD MY WINGS UNDER THE COVER!

HE HE HE

FLAP FLAP

SEE? WINGS!

WHAT'S GOING TO HAPPEN NEXT?! I MEAN THE NEXT VOLUME. (HA HA)

SPECIAL THEATRE:

MAIN CHARACTER(S)

AS IT TURNS OUT, PEOPLE'S REACTIONS WERE MOSTLY CENTERED AROUND THE MINOR CHARACTERS.

NOTHING ABOUT THE MAIN CHARACTERS.

...

I'M NOT BEING COCKY!!

IT'S NOT LIKE I WANT TO BE IN HERE!

AND WHY AM I THE ONLY ONE BEING ACCUSED ANYWAY?! SAKAMOTO'S JUST AS GUILTY AS I AM!

THEY CALLED HIM OUT, TOO.

ビクッ FREEZE

UGH, COME ON.

WOULD YOU QUIT WHINING? CHARACTERS HAVE CERTAIN ROLES THEY HAVE TO FILL.

THAT'S RIGHT. AND YOUR ROLE IS TO GET PICKED ON.

WHAT?! THAT'S CRAP...

WELL, HE DOESN'T COUNT SINCE HE'S AKIRA.
YEAH, WE'RE COOL WITH AKIRA.
TOTALLY.

ホ WHEW ッ...

WAIT, WHY?! THAT'S *FAVORITISM!* SAKAMOTO WAS EVEN IN THE SIDE STORY!
SO HOW COME *I'M* THE ONE WHO HAS TO BE DISCIPLINED?! I WON'T STAND FOR THIS!!

SPECIAL THEATRE:

STUDENT COUNCIL MEMBERS

AS IT TURNS OUT, THE PRESIDENT IS INCREDIBLY POPULAR!

HELLO! I'M ARISADA-- PRESIDENT AND, UNEXPECTEDLY, THE MOST POPULAR.
MY FIRST NAME IS SHUUYA.
WHY THANK YOU!

LET'S JUST CALL IT FATE(?) THAT I'M POPULAR. THERE WERE SOME STRONG DELUSIONS AMONGST EVERYONE'S OPINIONS.

THINGS LIKE WHAT RELATIONSHIP I HAVE WITH NATASHOU, WHAT'S GOING ON WITH ME AND THE COUNCIL MEMBERS...

OH!

SOME READERS ALSO WANTED TO KNOW IF I'D HAD ANY EXCHANGES WITH SAKAMOTO'S ELDER BROTHER.

FHN

AND I SAY TO YOU ALL, AREN'T YOU FORGETTING THAT THIS IS A ***MIKIYO TSUDA PRODUCTION?***

はっはっは,

HN HN

EVERY TIME I LET THIS GUY TALK, HE ALWAYS BECOMES THE MAIN CHAR-ACTER...

THERE WERE ALSO THOSE WHO WANTED TO SEE MY CHARMING SELF AS A PRINCESS.
AS MY COSTUME THEME WAS TRADITIONAL JAPANESE.
IT WAS ACTUALLY SUPPOSED TO BE INCLUDED IN A FLASHBACK SCENE,
BUT IN A HURRY TO MEET HER DEADLINE, THE ARTIST FORGOT ALL ABOUT IT...
WHAT A FOOL.
KA-THOK

SO, WITHOUT FURTHER ADO, HERE IS THE **GRAND UNVEILING.**

HERE HE IS IN A LONG-SLEEVED KIMONO.

WILL THIS DO, EVERYBODY ...?

SHHHING スイャッ
AHH! DON'T PUT ON FAKE GLASSES!!
THAT'S CHEATING!
WHAT DO YOU THINK? MORE CHARACTERS WITH GLASSES.

SPECIAL THEATRE END

PRIVATE DIARY 1

CRIPPLING BLOW

NEAR THE END OF SUMMER, THE BOOKSTORE I OFTEN WENT TO CLOSED DOWN.

SORRY, WE'RE ACTUALLY CLOSING DOWN...

WHA...

SO SHOCKED SHE CAN'T SAY ANYTHING.

THANKS FOR SHOPPING HERE...

I'D BEEN GOING THERE EVER SINCE I MOVED TO TOKYO. THEY GOT BOOKS EARLY AND HAD A GOOD SELECTION OF THINGS I LIKED, SO I WAS **ABSOLUTELY STUNNED** THAT THE STORE WAS CLOSING.

GSHH

NO... IT CAN'T BE...

GSHH

GSH

NOW THE WHOLE REASON I MOVED ALL THE WAY OUT HERE IS GONE!!

I'VE BEEN HERE FOR LIKE A YEAR! WHY IS IT CLOSING?

HUH?! IT'S NOT BECAUSE *I'M* HERE?!

EIKI LIVES ON THE OTHER SIDE OF THE STATION FROM ME.

SOMEONE... PLEASE... TELL ME WHERE THERE'S A BOOKSTORE WITH A GOOD SELECTION OF BOY'S LOVE NOVELS...

MY SOURCE OF ENERGY... ALL GONE...

I CAN'T POWER MYSELF UP CLOSE-BY ANYMORE...

HNG

HNG

HNNG

I THINK I MIGHT MOVE. (HA HA)

四コマ劇場

4-PANEL COMIC THEATRE

TSUDA-BEAR

MY MANGA ARTIST FRIEND
EIKI BUNNY
EIKI EIKI

PRIVATE DIARY 2

FASCINATING PANTS STORE

I WENT WITH MY FRIEND EIKI TO THE PANTS STORE SHE LIKES.
IT'S RIGHT HERE?! IT'S LIKE 100 FEET FROM MY HOUSE!
IT WAS AMAZINGLY ONLY A 30-SECOND WALK FROM MY PLACE.
YEP!
IT'S SO CLOSE AND I'VE NEVER BEEN.

AND THE PANTS THERE HAD INTERESTING DESIGNS WITH LOTS OF PATTERNS. THEY HAD A GOOD SELECTION.
ONES WITH LACES IN THE BACK
AND PATTERNS
AND MIXED COLORS
PANTS WITH DIFFERENT FABRIC IN FRONT AND BACK.
I WANTED SO MANY OF THEM, BUT I THOUGHT, "THERE'S NO WAY MY FAT BODY WOULD FIT INTO THOSE." SO I GAVE UP.
SO COOL...
はぁ~ SIGH

THEN...
THESE ARE ALL IMPORTS, SO THEY CAN STRETCH A LITTLE.
YOU'LL FIT FINE.
THAT'S WHY I CAN WEAR THEM.
WHAT? REALLY?!
WHEN I HEARD THAT, I ALMOST HALF-BELIEVED HER...
わぁー WAAAH!
THEY FIT! THEY FIT ME!!
MY UGLY BUTT AND MY FAT THIGHS DON'T STAND OUT! INCREDIBLE!!

SO I ENDED UP BUYING EVEN MORE THERE THAN EIKI DID, AND WE BOTH WENT HOME.
WHEN I SUGGESTED THAT PLACE YOU DIDN'T SEEM INTERESTED AT ALL...
WELL, I DIDN'T THINK THAT IF *YOU* COULD WEAR THEM THAT IT MEANT *I* COULD, TOO.
AFTER THAT, I STARTED GOING TO THE PANTS STORE A LOT.
BOO BOO
WE'RE NOT THE SAME SIZE.
SATISFIED
ゴッ EVERY-
ソリ THING

PRIVATE DIARY 3

FASCINATING BUTT

THE PANTS STORE EIKI SHOWED ME BECAME ONE OF MY FAVORITE STORES.
AND AT THE SAME TIME CAME MY DESIRE TO HAVE A **BEAUTIFUL BUTT AND SEXY LEGS!**
THIS WON'T DO... I BOUGHT CUTE PANTS, BUT THIS BUTT... THESE LEGS... THEY'RE SO UGLY!
OHHH

SO I DECIDED TO TRY DOING ONE OF THE MANY EXERCISE ROUTINES YOU CAN FIND ON JUST ABOUT ANY CHANNEL THESE DAYS.
TO BE HONEST, I TEND TO GIVE UP ON THINGS EASILY, SO I WAS WORRIED THAT I WOULDN'T KEEP AT IT...
I'D BETTER RECORD IT.

EVEN NOW, MY PANTS HOVER IN THE DISTANCE, DRIVING ME ON LIKE A CARROT LEADING A HORSE.
I WILL... I **WILL** WEAR THESE PANTS WELL...
DURING WORK, WHILE MY ASSISTANTS ARE FAST ASLEEP, I TOIL AWAY AT IT ALONE.

I REALLY JUST DON'T WANT PEOPLE SEEING ME DO THIS KIND OF THING.
I KINDA FEEL LIKE A FREAK BEHIND THE CURTAIN.
ALSO, WALKING TO EXERCISE YOUR BUTT WORKS LIKE MAGIC.
AND YOUR ABS!
はふー HFFF
はふー HFFF

PRIVATE DIARY 4

EVEN IF THEY'RE LONG...

I WENT AND BOUGHT A SUIT TO WEAR AT A FRIEND'S WED-DING.

WHEN I TRIED IT ON, THE LADY AT THE STORE SAID...

OH MY, MA'AM, YOU'VE GOT LONG LEGS.

WE'LL HAVE TO ALTER THE PANTS.

...

ACTUALLY, I'VE HEARD THIS MANY TIMES IN THE PAST...

FROM MY CLUB ADVIS-OR IN JUNIOR HIGH...

DO YOU HAPPEN TO HAVE LONG LEGS, TSUDA?

HAPPEN TO?

EVEN FROM THE LADY AT THAT PANTS STORE ...

OH, WOW! THEY FIT PERFECTLY! YOU MUST HAVE LONG LEGS.

I HEAR THE SAME THING EVERY TIME I SHOP FOR CLOTHES...

I MIGHT HAVE LONG LEGS, BUT WITH **FAT THIGHS AND AN UGLY BUTT** YOU CAN'T EVEN TELL...

IF THEY DON'T LOOK NICE, THERE'S NO POINT IN HAVING LONG LEGS.

きぃー

GRR! IF I COULD JUST DO SOMETHING ABOUT MY THIGHS AND MY BUTT...!!

FUME

I MUST KEEP EXER-CISING!

PRIVATE DIARY 5

MAYBE IF I ASK NICELY...

I'M ALWAYS GIVING THE POST OFFICE NEAR MY HOME A TOUGH TIME.

ガラ GACHAK

ガラ GACHAK

ガラ GACHAK

LIKE GIVING THEM EIGHT FULL BOXES AT ONCE.

THEN ONE DAY AT THE POST OFFICE... ONE OF THE CLERKS DROPPED A BOMB ON ME.

フフフ HE HE HE

I LOOKED AROUND AND BOUGHT SOME OF YOUR COMICS.

COULD I HAVE YOUR AUTOGRAPH?

ARE YOU SERIOUS?!

I DIDN'T WANT THEM TO KNOW I WAS A MANGA ARTIST, BUT I REALLY DIDN'T WANT THEM TO KNOW WHAT TYPE OF DRAWINGS I DO...

HOW? WHERE DID SHE FIND OUT...?

I DON'T USE ANYTHING BUT MY REAL NAME HERE...

OH, GOD... I HOPE THEY HAVEN'T READ MY TAISHI ZAOU BOOKS!

I ENDED UP GIVING AUTOGRAPHS TO THE OTHER CLERKS AND THE CUSTOMERS WAITING BEHIND ME, TOO.

キュキュッ SKRIK SKRIK

I HAVE ONE MORE IF YOU DON'T MIND.

>SIGH< ...IF POSSIBLE, I WOULD HAVE LIKED TO KEEP IT SECRET...

PRIVATE DIARY 6
I THINK YOU'VE GOT IT WRONG...
WHEN I WENT TO THE LOCAL CONVEN-IENCE STORE, I RAN INTO A CLERK FROM THE POST OFFICE.
OH. HI, MISS TSUDA
AH!
HI, CLERK.
WHY... WHY DID IT HAVE TO BE HERE...?
WHY NOT SOME OTHER STORE?
AHH, DON'T LOOK AT ME...
EEEK
I DON'T HAVE MAKEUP ON...
I'D JUST WOKEN UP, AND HADN'T WASHED MY FACE. I HADN'T EVEN FIXED MY HAIR. I GOT SO UPSET THAT SOMEONE I KNEW SAW ME WHEN I WAS SO UNKEMPT.
MISS TSUDA, DESPITE BEING A MANGA ARTIST, YOU'VE ALWAYS BEEN QUITE CLEAN. IT'S REALLY IMPRES-SIVE.
HUH?!
IT'S JUST THESE PANTS...
I WAS TOTALLY SUR-PRISED.
A LADY AT THAT PANTS STORE SAID SOME-THING SIMILAR TO ME TOO.
WHAT DOES THIS MEAN? IF THEY SAY I'M CLEAN WHEN I'M LIKE THIS...
DOES THAT MEAN PEOPLE THINK MANGA ARTISTS ARE NORMALLY REALLY DIRTY?
...
IT'S SIMPLY NOT TRUE (HA HA).
WELL, NOT FOR EVERYONE.
IT'S ONLY WHEN WE HAVE TO MEET A DEADLINE.
PRIVATE DIARY 7
PEOPLE ARE...
I HEARD AN ALARM CLOCK GOING OFF SOME-WHERE, SO I WENT TO GO FIND OUT WHERE IT WAS COMING FROM, AND FOLLOWED THE SOUND OUTSIDE.
HM?
WHERE IS IT?
SOUNDS LIKE IT'S OVER THERE...
HANG ON...
IS SOME-THING... BURN-ING?
SNIFF SNIFF
TURNS OUT IT WAS THE FIRE ALARM.
RIRIRIRI
F- F- F- FIRE?!
I'M SO STUPID. WITHOUT EVEN THINKING, I STARTED LOOKING FOR THE OFF SWITCH.
THEN I WAS RUN-NING WITH ONLY THE KEY...
ONCE I GOT TO A SAFE SPOT, I REALIZED I SHOULD HAVE BROUGHT IMPORTANT STUFF LIKE MY WALLET, MY CELL PHONE, OR MY BANK RECORDS.
UH OH!
THIS DOESN'T HELP ME AT ALL!
I UNDERSTOOD WELL, THEN, THAT EVEN WHEN I THINK I KNOW WHAT I'M DOING, I REALLY CAN'T DO THE THINGS I SHOULD.
NOTHING COMES TO MIND...
I THOUGHT I COULD STAY CALMER THAN THAT...
IN THE END, THE FIRE ALARM WENT OFF BECAUSE SOMEONE ON THE FLOOR BELOW LEFT AN EMPTY POT ON THE STOVE. FORTUNATELY IT DIDN'T END IN DISASTER.
THANK GOODNESS!
MMM
MN
IF MY PLACE HAD BURNED DOWN, WE WOULDN'T HAVE BEEN ABLE TO PUT OUT VOLUME ②...

4-PANEL COMIC THEATRE ✸ END

THANK

YOU

SO

MUCH

FOR

READING!!

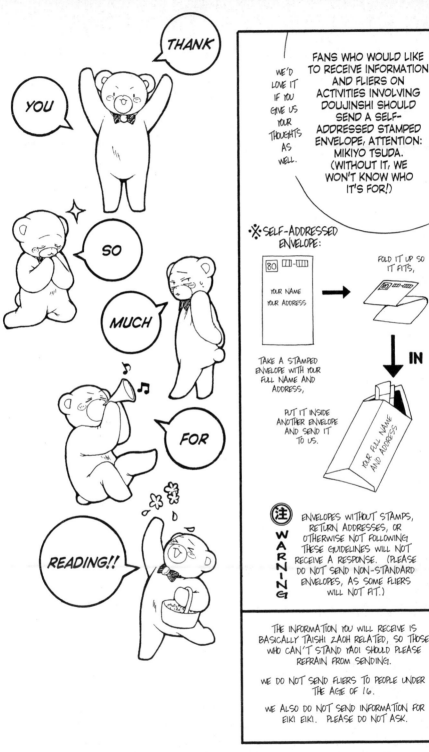

FANS WHO WOULD LIKE TO RECEIVE INFORMATION AND FLIERS ON ACTIVITIES INVOLVING DOUJINSHI SHOULD SEND A SELF-ADDRESSED STAMPED ENVELOPE, ATTENTION: MIKIYO TSUDA. (WITHOUT IT, WE WON'T KNOW WHO IT'S FOR!)

WE'D LOVE IT IF YOU GIVE US YOUR THOUGHTS AS WELL.

※SELF-ADDRESSED ENVELOPE:

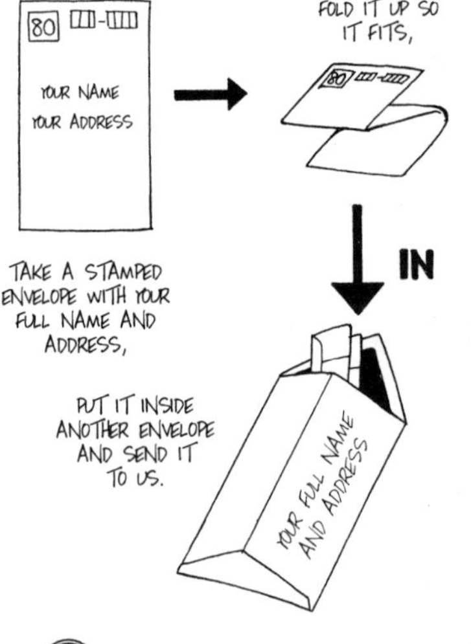
80
YOUR NAME
YOUR ADDRESS
FOLD IT UP SO IT FITS,
80
IN
TAKE A STAMPED ENVELOPE WITH YOUR FULL NAME AND ADDRESS,
PUT IT INSIDE ANOTHER ENVELOPE AND SEND IT TO US.
YOUR FULL NAME AND ADDRESS

注 WARNING

ENVELOPES WITHOUT STAMPS, RETURN ADDRESSES, OR OTHERWISE NOT FOLLOWING THESE GUIDELINES WILL NOT RECEIVE A RESPONSE. (PLEASE DO NOT SEND NON-STANDARD ENVELOPES, AS SOME FLIERS WILL NOT FIT.)

THE INFORMATION YOU WILL RECEIVE IS BASICALLY TAISHI ZAOH RELATED, SO THOSE WHO CAN'T STAND YAOI SHOULD PLEASE REFRAIN FROM SENDING.

WE DO NOT SEND FLIERS TO PEOPLE UNDER THE AGE OF 16.

WE ALSO DO NOT SEND INFORMATION FOR EIKI EIKI. PLEASE DO NOT ASK.

THE DAY OF REVOLUTION

MIKIYO TSUDA

♂ Male...

Or Female...? ♀

What's a gender-confused
kid supposed to do?

DMP

DIGITAL MANGA PUBLISHING

ISBN# 1-56970-889-4 $12.95

La Esperança
Despite young Georges popularity, he has never been able to truly forge a close bond with others. That is, of course, until he met Robert!
But after time, will Georges come to regret it?
Mystery surrounds him and only a tragic clue from the past may provide the answer.
La Esperança
1
Yaoi Manga
DMP
VOL. 1 ISBN# 1-56970-933-5 $12.95
VOL. 2 ISBN# 1-56970-932-7 $12.95
VOL. 3 ISBN # 1-56970-931-9 $12.95
VOL. 4 ISBN# 1-56970-930-0 $12.95
VOL. 5 ISBN# 1-56970-929-7 $12.95
VOL. 6 ISBN# 978-1569708484 $12.95
VOL. 7 ISBN# 978-1569708309 $12.95
June™
junemanga.com

Enchanter
IZUMI KAWACHI
...lighter and more humorous [than] Full Metal Alchemist...
- Active Anime
DMP

THE Moon AND Sandals
月とサンダル
Vol. 1
THE MOON & SANDALS 1 © 1996 Fumi Yoshinaga. All rights reserved. First published in Japan in 1996 by HOBUNSHA CO., LTD., Tokyo
SEE ME AFTER CLASS!
June™ by DMP

ISBN# 978-1-56970-802-9 SRP $12.95

As a newly appointed high school teacher, Ida has yet to gain confidence in his abilities. His insecurity grows worse when he feels someone staring intensely at him during class. The piercing eyes belong to a tall, intimidating student – Koichi Kobayashi. What exactly should Ida do about it? Is it discontent that fuels Kobayashi's sultry gaze… or could it be something else?

Written and Illustrated by:
Fumi Yoshinaga

junemanga.com

Digital Manga Inc. presents...
POP JAPAN CULTURE
Anime and Manga
THE ULTIMATE TOUR!
サロンパス
POP
ポップ
JAPAN
TRAVEL
For reservations or inquiries, please contact:
Pop Japan Travel: (310) 817-8010 Fax: (310) 817-8018
E-mail: travel@popjapantravel.com Web: www.popjapantravel.com

This is the back of the book!
Start from the other side.

NATIVE MANGA readers read manga from *right to left*.

*If you run into our **Native Manga** logo on any of our books... you'll know that this manga is published in it's true original native Japanese right to left reading format, as it was intended. Turn to the other side of the book and start reading from right to left, top to bottom.*

Follow the diagram to see how its done.
Surf's Up!